COMMIT
TO
Change

NEVA WELSH

WESTBOW
PRESS®
A DIVISION OF THOMAS NELSON
& ZONDERVAN

Copyright © 2020 Neva Welsh.

All rights reserved. No part of this book may be used or reproduced by any means, graphic, electronic, or mechanical, including photocopying, recording, taping or by any information storage retrieval system without the written permission of the author except in the case of brief quotations embodied in critical articles and reviews.

This book is a work of non-fiction. Unless otherwise noted, the author and the publisher make no explicit guarantees as to the accuracy of the information contained in this book and in some cases, names of people and places have been altered to protect their privacy.

WestBow Press books may be ordered through booksellers or by contacting:

WestBow Press
A Division of Thomas Nelson & Zondervan
1663 Liberty Drive
Bloomington, IN 47403
www.westbowpress.com
1 (866) 928-1240

Because of the dynamic nature of the Internet, any web addresses or links contained in this book may have changed since publication and may no longer be valid. The views expressed in this work are solely those of the author and do not necessarily reflect the views of the publisher, and the publisher hereby disclaims any responsibility for them.

Any people depicted in stock imagery provided by Getty Images are models, and such images are being used for illustrative purposes only.
Certain stock imagery © Getty Images.

Author Photo - Christopher Analista, owner of Reckless Love Media

All Scripture quotations are taken from The Holy Bible, New International Version®, NIV® Copyright © 1973, 1978, 1984, 2011 by Biblica, Inc.® Used by permission. All rights reserved worldwide.

ISBN: 978-1-9736-8528-9 (sc)
ISBN: 978-1-9736-8529-6 (hc)
ISBN: 978-1-9736-8527-2 (e)

Library of Congress Control Number: 2020902809

Print information available on the last page.

WestBow Press rev. date: 2/17/2020

Dedication

To the one who is my all in all and to whom I owe everything, my Father, God, who created me, my Lord and Savior Jesus Christ, who paid my debt, and the Holy Spirit, who is my counselor and comforter. May your words speak to whomever needs to hear, and may they produce the desired outcome. To you be all the praise, glory, and honor!

The beginning is the most important part of the work.
—Plato, 429–347 BCE

Preface

Here I sit with deep inner conviction, trying to overcome paralyzing fear that desires to hold me captive. Is it the day, the hour, or even the year that propels to breakthrough, regardless of the cost? The ache in a physical body as one labors to be free is inferior to the ache in the heart and soul that cries for freedom. The physical must submit to the deeper call within to progress. One must follow and hope to complete their dream or assignment and mine was to write something meaningful. What an impossible task when compared to so many capable, highly intelligent, and experienced writers, yet the nagging and push to try would not depart. A journey of obedience is in progress.

The intent of this book is to help those in similar patterns of pain, emptiness, insecurity, guilt, shame, disappointments, anger, rejection, abuse, addictions, loneliness, hate, and any other human frailties. The goal is to look together at difficult issues, discover the way of escape, and move into freedom. We are encouraged to accept and realize that burying, hiding, or ignoring issues that need resolution will rob us of energy, joy, and contentment. It is not a quick fix or a one-time solution but a powerful realization of who you are and of your uniqueness and significance. The final hope is to accept your true identity and help others through rough times to victory.

I am a simple woman. I was an active child with a wild imagination at times. I am one of four siblings. We were blessed with wonderful parents whom we all miss and believe we will see again. I was married at a young age to the most wonderful man and so perfect for me. We have four wonderful children and their spouses who have blessed us with amazing additions—grandchildren and even great-grandchildren! Life has been filled with travel due to my husband's military career and the joy of travel.

I remember as a little girl loving to tell stories, and my mother told me that I kept the owner and employees of our local grocery store quite entertained. I would also sing for them but long ago gave up the dream of singing aloud with anyone within earshot. However, the desire to express myself and share with others grew. I wrote a short skit in 5th or 6th grade that was performed on our little school stage. We giggled; we shared thoughts and memories, and then I moved away due to my father's employment relocation. I am both outgoing but also at times reserved.

A few times over the years friends or acquaintances would say, "you should write a book." However, once, when I shared with a local leader, he looked at me and said, "That is nothing but pride." Something died in me that evening, and something took root that should not have. I was already so afraid of the thought of writing, but now I was accused of something far worse than fear or insecurity—foolishness and pride. I am aware that all battle pride, but this cut deep. I ignored a gift and accepted doubt.

After years of when hope and a dream seemed dead, the thoughts and comments of well-wishers persisted that I should write. I again shared with someone close to me. The comment back was, "With so many books, how do you write something that someone would buy and read?" I did not know, so the dream was buried even deeper.

However, something was powerfully awakened within me while I was attending an Aglow conference in November of 2014. I was quietly sitting alone, waiting for the meeting to start. A woman came and sat down beside me and said, "I believe, God told me to ask you, when are you going to write the book?" I could barely look at her. It was very jarring. I took her name and number, for she lived hundreds of miles away, maybe even a thousand. I had never seen or met her before. I did hug her and thank her, and deep emotions were stirred within me. I cannot find her name, address, or the additional words that I wrote down that she spoke to me that evening, or I would quote them verbatim.

Close to the same time that this incident happened, a friend from my past of over thirty years connected with me, thanks to the technology of today. She called to say hello and to tell me how much all the things that I had written to her over the years meant to her personally. She shared that she had kept every card and note that I had ever given or sent to her. She stated how they still speak to her and how some things that I had shared or told her long ago were still so memorable and precious to her. We were both thankful for our friendship and happy that she had reconnected us.

I, again, was a little shaken. I felt a twinge of guilt for not being obedient if I were to write, fear of trying, shame for believing lies, and for allowing them to lock me in a state of not following my dream. What a crossroad I found myself at again, so many years after the original dream to write was alive. So, here we are at the junction of a beginning that is unfolding in the following pages.

The examples that follow are occurrences, lessons, or situations that I have seen, learned, heard, or personally experienced. I hope to learn more as I begin this monumental task with one small step or stroke on the keyboard. I hope you will gain some insights and enjoy the attempt of expression.

Neva

Acknowledgments

I would never be able to adequately thank my husband for all the love and faith that he had in me to begin and complete this endeavor. He has labored with me and has spent hours editing, proofing, sharing suggestions, and handling technical issues. His love, support, and encouragement are immeasurable. Thank you to my beloved husband, Don.

To my awesome children and their families, who have shared in the journey and are precious gifts and blessings, I say thank you.

To my precious friend, Sharyn, who was so determined to reconnect and did. God used her to encourage me to write; thank you, Sharyn.

To my dear Christian family who loves me and has lifted me in prayer, I say thank you.

And to the stranger who approached me and related that she believed that God told her to tell me, you are to write a book. What an impetus to begin! Thank you for your obedience.

What profound support and life lessons each of you have provided. You are true treasures and awesome gifts to me. Thank you from the deepest recess of my heart. You are part of the journey.

section 1
BEGINNINGS

The secret of getting ahead is getting started.

—Mark Twain, 1835–1910

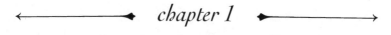

chapter 1
WHO ARE WE?

The recording of thoughts and ideas may not be to just share personal events but an inner drive to gain and share insight. Life is full of twists and turns and ups and downs. Mistakes are made, consequences dealt, and victories celebrated—all mingled in a lifetime.

Some of my personal life will be in the mix as I try to relate how to avoid pitfalls, be alert to warning signs, and identify and embrace ancient guideposts and wisdom.

Life resembles a huge cauldron filled with wonderful emotions of joy, hope, love, peace, compassion, dreams, and trust, and yet the mix is darkened with shattered dreams, lies, and deceptions. Who is stirring the pot? What causes such turmoil? Outlook on life becomes clouded by the constant frenzy of trying to understand and control the mixture.

Some seem to be sailing successfully through life with no problems but have inner struggles and battles that no one sees. Others' battles may be evident to those who surround the individual. Cataloging others in a "less than us" frame of mind helps hold our own monsters at bay. However, this is a double-edged sword when we realize others are "better than us." We spiral down or find another way to fight the battle for normalcy and wholeness. Judgment and evaluation of another's status is a defective tool used to form a warped frame of identity. It is ineffective and divisive.

How do we survive and relate to one another and become unified instead of erecting barriers? We long to manage life skillfully and enjoy all of it. We need adequate tools and new ways to successfully face life and its challenges.

For years, I have been involved in reaching out to inmates in a state prison. I have yet to meet one whose childhood dream was to be incarcerated. Yet they know and nod to the truth that if they had not been apprehended, they would be in a worse state or even dead. They hate where they are but at the same time recognize it as a lifeline. There is a ray of hope that wells up inside. Life is full of such dichotomies.

Life's choices sometimes result in cruel shackles of addiction, hate, revenge, or whatever evil strangles the freedom of the soul. Incarceration offers a chance, when they are at total brokenness and desiring change, to break the chains of bondage. The journey of new surroundings and circumstances begins—a circle of life.

In a prison setting, adjustments must be made very quickly, and adjustments are undertaken to survive. However, this is not just about adjusting but flourishing in life's challenges. We do not want to be crushed by our circumstances or rolled over repeatedly by the same traps, so how do we succeed? Where do we find strength, acceptance, love, and security? How does anyone start over again?

The desire is to identify some of the traps, the lies, and the strategies that encumber many of us as we try to find our way to a productive, fulfilling life. We are more alike than we realize—whether we are rich or poor, young or old, educated or illiterate, a prisoner of a penal system or a prisoner of the soul. Life has many ways of opening our eyes to the truth of our commonalities, regardless of our backgrounds, ethnicities, or nationalities. Of course, we have heard or read this, but experience speaks louder than words. We have all failed to recognize faults, committed deception, or simply made wrong choices.

Sometimes we delve into the past trying to find answers. Others engage in group encounters, friends, drugs, alcohol, books, classes, exercise, and religion. Oh, how we try to find the thread that will unravel and expose the error so we can right it. Where is the key to unlocking all the mysteries so we might come away full of revelation and new purpose?

Each of the above solutions for finding answers holds its own traps.

We are hooked on an ideal path to solve the problem only to find more rules, more restrictions, more, more, more. Do more, change more, be more, and conform and adapt to the expectations of others who are also on our chosen path. Moreover, the wheel is spinning again. Many have tendencies to jump into action in their excitement or desperation and do not fully "test the waters." We may react to disillusionment and withdraw too quickly. We must learn to wait.

We do not gain all of the answers, but at least hopefully, we become more aware of some of the traps and solutions as we continue the search.

Many of us cannot—or do not—relate to one another's circumstances or even acknowledge the correlations. I have no remarkable points that will secure this identification of sameness, but I know we experience many commonalities. We can be oblivious to others' problems or pain when we are in a good season (self-absorbed). Alternatively, we can drown in sorrow over others' situations—including our own. Sometimes life is a wild ride.

Many are so wounded that they give up hope and enter a downward spiral that it may take years to escape. Left alone, feelings of anger and disappointment can lead to isolation, depression, or extreme judgment and prejudice. We need to be aware of these feelings and signs within and address our problems with eyes open, not succumbing to blindness.

New and different concepts are challenging. We want to understand, but it is scary leaving behind some "truths" and the pain of deception. We need something to hold on to; we need an anchor. We do not want to spin out of control. It is terrifying when everything we thought was true and right is questioned, examined, and shaken. What is happening? There are defects. Being hit with the frailties of humankind and its systems is an eye-opener—it is *revelational*.

It hurts when you discover concealed issues. Some of these discoveries have led many to hardened hearts and destructive ways. The discovery of impure motives and practices can shake you to your core. It wounds. It makes you question yourself and others. What is reality? What is true? Whenever and wherever humankind is involved, there is an imperfect core. Self has raised its ugly head and demanded its own way. Excuses abound, and the core becomes more and more stained.

We may engage in self-examination and in confrontation, hoping to understand what we may have misunderstood and plan to engage in effecting change. Sometimes this will work; it can also definitely backfire, and you will be stung with more poison and pain. How does one not "throw the baby out with the bathwater"?

What are some behavioral patterns that hurt so deeply, and how should we handle them? I hope that we can identify them as we proceed. Paralyzing fear is a roadblock, but fear can also be an impetus for change and a shield of protection.

How do we remain sensitive yet not overwhelmed? Let us seek the answers together.

The goal is to discover the best tool for the situation without yielding to any negative adherence. In the following pages, may we recognize pitfalls and discover effective solutions.

Onward.

The unexamined life is not worth living.

—Socrates, 469–399 BCE

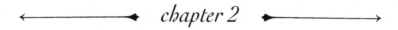

chapter 2
A SMALL BEGINNING

One of the first cyclical changes in human beginnings, over which we have no say or control, is when the sperm penetrates the ovum and life begins. Once the ova and the sperm complete their mission, another phase begins. Immediately, the fertilized ovum is embedded in the uterine wall, which had previously undergone changes to nourish and protect the new life. Spontaneous division and rapid multiplication occur with differentiation; a unique individual is developing.

The embryo is an original and continues to develop, and soon it is time for the infant to come forth. The baby presents through a previous one- to two-inch-thick muscular cylinder that has become an almost-perfect four-inch paper-thin circle. Alignment or proper positioning and forward progression are essential for an uninterrupted delivery.

In obstetrics, the period when the cervix is fully dilated and the baby is in the birth canal is known as *transition*—the most dangerous time of a normal labor for the mother and the infant. The infant's progression must continue, or its life is endangered. The cord, which has served as the lifeline, may be compressed in the narrow passageway, leading to a decreased supply of oxygen. There are many possible emergencies—dangerous blood loss, premature release of the placenta, vital-sign changes, complications with size—all of which affect the mother and the infant.

We all realize it is not always an easy or perfect labor and delivery, but the natural progress is for the baby to come forth through the canal in short order, and the reward of labor is celebrated.

However, multiple complications during delivery may occur. If the infant is not presenting headfirst but instead leads with its buttocks, foot, or shoulder, dilatation of the cervix may be hindered, and the risk of not being able to pass through the birth canal is increased. This is life-threatening. Blood pressure and blood supply may change drastically, presenting a danger to both the mother and infant. The health of the mother, her prenatal care history, and healthy habits are all vital to a successful birth. Nevertheless, the natural progression and textbook outline is a miraculous, innate response. Our bodies truly are amazing! Labor progresses to bring forth the fruit of its efforts regardless of outside happenings (e.g., wars, natural disasters, arguments).

Each beginning is unique and may or may not have been a desired occurrence. The newly created life can be highly anticipated, resented, grossly mistreated, and even destroyed. Great preparation can go into the welcome of the addition to an existing circle, or it may never be fully acknowledged or accepted. However, this baby will make itself known and join the cycle of life.

When the baby is expelled from its temporary home, the only one that the infant has known, everything familiar is left behind. The struggling little one is grabbed, rubbed, and the lifeline is cut. The previous home now discards everything that had sustained the fetus.

Now what? Uterine habitation is over. Expanded education begins. Thoughts, experiences, and perceptions form the basis of awareness. Every day, every year, thought patterns and behaviors are established, tried, expanded, neglected, or relegated to a designated file.

There are adherents to *embryo memory recall* of these events. I cannot testify to this specifically, but I do believe each life is affected by words and actions from conception onward.

Many studies support the idea that the personality of babies and their reactions to circumstances are related to prenatal conditions. It is obvious that unwanted or unsafe chemicals that enter the baby have long-lasting effects, so it is feasible that situations that invoke deep emotions affect not only the mother but also the life within the womb.

We did not choose who our parents would be, and maybe they did not even choose each other. They may have or have not wanted us, but here we are. Many of us are still dragging baggage that we picked up early in life, which is still trying to control our destiny.

Likes, dislikes, patterns, dreams, and expectations affect and fill us tremendously in our first young years of life. How we interpret and respond to others and our environment continues to mold us. We form alliances that support our longings. We can have imaginary friends or a big social circle of friends with high hopes and dreams or sit in despair. However, perceptions are established and included in our circles or boundaries.

We can enjoy life or dread it every day. What an internal battle. Sometimes the beauty of our world takes our breath away—a newborn's soft skin, birds singing, trees budding, snowcapped mountains—joy is everywhere. Life is full of fun and exciting moments; one is welcoming a newborn, while another is watching someone becoming a man or woman in his or her own right and a gift to society.

Disappointments may manifest at every junction of life. The baby has major problems, finances are desperate, stress is high, he or she did not make the team or get that promotion. How we hurt for those we love. Peer pressure may turn your child against your teaching. You watch as they turn away, too often with angry looks and remarks. How will your heart ever heal? How will theirs? How will we find our way back together? How does a shattered marriage recover? Betrayal, abandonment, and judgment by others leave scars etched on a heart. How can one breathe again? Beauty and awe are all around, but you can only say, "I know it is there, but I cannot see it or feel it." Depression squelches joy.

A soul cries for its children or loved ones. A heart breaks for them, for the path they have chosen is filled with pain and anguish. You can see the pitfalls but are powerless to change the direction. However, deep within, hope stirs. Somehow, you hang on. Somehow, you know it will be okay. Somehow, the spinning out of control will slow down, and balance returns. The one who promised until death parts is estranged, but still, you know life goes on. There is something more, something deeper.

I share the beautiful example of a child being brought into this world because it is something, if you are reading this, you have experienced in one way or another. I do believe there is a pattern that was intended from the beginning for this process of life coming forth, but it has been so skewed or distorted from the original plan that we easily overlook or deny the originator.

How do we perceive our journey through changes in life? How do we naturally go through transition into change? The transition from prenatal life to outside life is a vulnerable and sometimes dangerous time. What a new scene: bright lights, cold environment, noisy, and where are the boundaries? Leaving one site to a totally new arena can evoke myriad emotions throughout life. It is called *change*, and often we have little or no control over the timing or the change. Change and all its implications touch all of our lives. We can resist, hate, tolerate, or embrace. Some changes are welcome, some catastrophic. Nevertheless, we all face it in one way or another.

In childbirth, there is a preset bodily response to propel the process. How do we establish patterns to successfully transition in life's circumstances in the healthiest and most productive way? We often overlook the transition. Sometimes, we jump at the chance of change, or we drag our feet and dig in our heels. Change also has a habit of arriving unexpectedly and even being unwelcomed. How do we best prepare to move and transition from one state or place to another?

Remember, in the order of progression for change, transition is the most vulnerable period. Once established in the new place, you have a new bearing and a new set of perimeters with a learning curve or adjustment. What happened during the "transition phase" determines how well the adaptation in the new area progresses.

So again, how do we improve or recognize and prepare for transitions in our lives? I believe this is critical to our adjustments in life and for smoother passage.

I have shortened or hastened transitions, ignored or denied transitions, prolonged or delayed transitions, obstructed or hindered transitions. How about you? How has it affected your life and the lives of others? We are bombarded with information and helpful solutions until we can hear no more. Yet something is stirring inside. Is it hope?

Where does this hope come from? I know that it is attacked. Lies swarm around your ears. You see it in statistics, you hear it from friendly advisors, and you can see failures, death, heartache. All around are shattered hopes, newscasts filled with all kinds of horrors. You want to hide, not hear, see, or listen to anyone or anything. You want shelter, protection for yourself and your loved ones.

Still, something is trying to push itself up on the inside. It is hope! Hope arises and leads us on and through the tough times. Somehow, you know life is a gift and good can still come from what seems to be gone forever. Reflect on the small beginning, and remember that whatever has occurred in your life has not destroyed the hope within. More is to come about renewing and reviving hope.

chapter 3

BOUNDARY CIRCLES

Boundaries diminish, fade, and change and are vital wheels in our lives, orchestrated by whom we let in, whom we shut out, who depart by choice, whom we let go. Boundaries are established but are never permanent.

Our circles are illuminators of what we think, what we know, what we *think* we know, and what we believe. The treasure chest of our understanding travels with us on our journey, but sometimes it bursts. It can fall away with a crash or with subtle changes that sometimes go unnoticed. Nevertheless, a boundary has been radically readjusted.

Broad circles fill with many people and ideas and may shrink as others move away, or as we do, due to life's circumstances or values. However, for a season, we shine like a bright light in a dark place and flow seamlessly together. Our center is clear, and the entire periphery united. Then suddenly, an invasive thought, person, or event shatters our bubble, or it painfully stretches it as we struggle to regain balance.

One contemplates, *Where am I, where have I been, and where am I going?* Core values and relationships are challenged. We grab hold of the stabilizer, perhaps not even recognizing who or what it is, but regardless of how many times life spins out of orbit, it realigns us.

As a young girl, I was given a diary, as many young girls are. The mystical hype surrounding "the diary" never caught me. I tried and would hide it and lock it, as expected, but it fell flat and was soon discarded.

As a young woman, the longing to pour out my soul resurged, and I began to write. This time, I decided to correspond with my Creator. I figured He knew me pretty well, and without trying to be superficial or fake, since He would recognize that, I began to explode with emotion in a safe place (home, in a little book)—in a very private boundary. An elementary attempt to understand and maintain balance was developing and evolving.

I recently dug my "journals," or sheets of crumpled paper, out of boxes. My goodness, how enlightening the review was. They were boring at times. Other times they were filled with raw emotions. It marked out a trail of tears, of hope, of failures, of successes, and of surprises—all on the path of life poignantly recorded.

So, what have I learned? What was the purpose? Was time and effort wasted? What meaning is there in all these records of daily joys and struggles? Is there any value beyond the amazing portal of communication that it provided me? I do believe expression and evaluating matters is a step in growth, regardless of how simple it may appear. The journals served as a catharsis and were crucial in my development and balance. I know that what is cathartic for one is not for another. However, exploring and recording daily events and examining them were instrumental for my growth and understanding. There are many avenues to personal enlightenment, and the ways are limitless.

Expressing thoughts and sharing emotions and possibilities, along with seeing and recognizing outcomes, is instrumental in establishing acceptable borders. Without guidelines for life choices, one risks being adrift, like a lost ship, without an anchor in rough waters. Boundaries should protect, secure, and allow abundant room for simultaneous growth and exploration.

Our outlook and ways of facing life are affected by words, environment, and the behaviors of others, starting at a very young age with your family dynamics. Coping mechanisms are numerous and intertwined. If insecurity or unworthiness is rooted deep within you, there are many "sucker" attachments. Fear, doubt, comparison, anger, judgment, and many other negative emotions help define your methods of response.

Many positive inputs also define your adaptations to life. The attachments, whether helpful or harmful, flow so smoothly together that we do not even notice the seamless cloth of endless responses.

We may not always be able to identify the source when an emotion that is a major component of our personality is established. We hear things like "It is just who I am," or "I am just like my father," but we are all responsible for what we allow to define us. Genes may give us blue eyes or red hair, but I am not aware of an excuse gene!

I speak from experience when I talk about forming an identity with rejection and unworthiness that I had to choose to overcome. I was aware of it from a very young age, and it became a part of me. When I became aware of some of my beginnings, I gained insight, but it was a long battle to overcome this stronghold in my life.

Doctors tried to convince my mother to abort me due to her health and severe pregnancy problems. She refused; however, in the last trimester, she was ready to end the pregnancy, but it was too late. Complications on the delivery table called for emergency intervention, and my father had to decide for my mother's life or mine. Of course, he chose his bride and the mother of their first little girl, but thankfully, we both made it.

Is this when the roots of rejection, insecurity, and lack of value entered my soul? There are many theories out there that would support such a claim. Nevertheless, I believe that we all have choices. I was in a loving family and was a wanted child, but I was not able to grab all the goodness and dispose of the garbage at such an immature time in my life. I held on to negative comments and lies. Teasing also can be a cruel method of tearing one down. I tried to ignore and block unwanted thoughts and allow love and acceptance to rule, but I assimilated flawed concepts into my life pattern and had battles to wage, as I believe we all do.

As stated above, we risk being adrift without an anchor in rough waters. We need our good boundaries for our heart, soul, and mind to protect and secure us in fertile ground, for successful growth and exploration. However, often, we try to overcompensate and try hard to please others, which may stress our boundaries.

Thank God for those who see past personal flaws and recognize life's spark of uniqueness in each individual and their potential. It seems as if the majority choose the easier road of judging. It makes me think of Maria in the *Sound of Music* and the phrase, "How do you solve a problem like Maria?" I believe many have sung a similar refrain over me. I was a little mischievous at times.

The flaws in our behavior and thought processes may be buried and temporarily conquered only to resurface. However, we are invited to an encounter that will help us understand. I hope our calling card arrives very soon.

chapter 4

CYCLES

Oh, the cycles we develop as coping mechanisms are numerous and intertwined. If insecurity is rooted deep within you, its root of fear and unbelief sustain the sucker attachments of unworthiness, comparison, and judgment. They go together so smoothly that we do not even sense or notice the insidious connection.

My mother's pregnancy with me was one of severe sickness, hospitalization, bedrest, injections, medications, and fighting for the continued pregnancy as doctors encouraged her to abort. As the extreme pain and nausea continued, month after month, eventually my mother begged the doctor to alleviate or to evacuate the womb to provide relief in her horrifying battle. However, it was too late. I was not aware of her desire to end the pregnancy until she was close to her own death. I believe she needed to share during the time that we were very close, and she knew we both deeply loved one another. She was free to be open and honest about her heartache and painful experience. I understood.

On the delivery table, as I shared previously, life-threatening complications arose. The obstetrician informed my father that only one of us could be saved. "You must make a decision: your wife or the baby." Of course, his wife was paramount to him, and the vote was cast. As stated, we both made it.

Many amazing new theories have revealed what the embryo and infant go through and absorb in the womb. I recall reading them or hearing about them at lectures, but I do not have clear recollection where I heard the theories. I see television ads and in-store offers for soothing music to play during pregnancy and recommendations that parents should talk and sing to their baby while still in the womb. This is to help prepare them for entering their new circle of life, to welcome them to the family unit, and to build a recognition of (especially the mother's) voice.

I do know that from a very young age, I suffered with deep feelings of rejection and fought many health battles. Was it linked to my mother's battle and my own experience during the gestation period?

Where do the roots of insecurity come from? We all have it in some measure, but mine was very deep. We can feel, receive, and know love, but sometimes it is so fleeting. Then we try to understand and search for reasons why that's so.

Personal security is affected negatively by the words and behaviors of others, through neglect, abandonment, bullying, comparisons, teasing, lies, and environmental circumstances. Our filters are immature, and we believe and assimilate into our core belief system or values flawed concepts that we are inferior and unlovable. ("There must be something wrong with me.")

To compensate and function as an active and loved individual, one tries so hard to please others, settle down, and remain within boundaries. Thank God for those who see past personal struggles, whether it is insecurity, rebellion, or the pressure of trying to please everyone, and instead recognize life's spark of uniqueness in each individual. However, unfortunately, many focus only on the shortcomings and see problems.

To help myself maintain balance and shake off insecurity and unworthiness, I would travel down my own road of perfection, and when I fell, a sharp detour was taken. This bumpy and deceptive detour road was called "Oh well, not as bad as ..." (my road of comparison and judgment) or "You will never make it" (my path of failure). The battle of insecurity would give relief through pride or a *better-than* or *not-as-bad-as* attitude! At this point, there would be only a temporary break, because the guilt of thinking that way would convict me, and then I felt lower than a worm. What kind of life is this?

Insecurity is a terrible stranglehold, full of fear, and has many tentacles. It is worth the battle to overcome to enjoy acceptance and security.

chapter 5

MERRY-GO-ROUND

Sometimes life is like a whirling merry-go-round, causing you to hang on for dear life when it spins rapidly. Feelings of excitement, fear, and maybe even nausea rise up, and you try to make sense of it all. Then, as it slows and goes at a more acceptable speed, which brings delight, you are so thankful for the thrill, for the change, and for the familiarity. As you jump off, your balance may be shaky, and you cannot walk in a straight line, but you quickly adapt and go on. Anticipation and fear await the next turn or ride in life.

Where does the saying come from that life is like a merry-go-round? Some days and nights, my mind is filled with fleeting thoughts jumbling around in my head. I feel like they are in a circular motion, like a supersonic merry-go-round. Often there is no identifiable order or sequence; it is like popcorn popping.

Balance is crucial in life. I do not even pretend to fully understand the perfect balance needed in our galaxy for life on earth to be sustained. I struggle with my own merry-go-round balance and the centrifugal force that would propel me flying out of orbit.

Sometimes that is how our life feels. We juggle acts to keep everything in order in our circle, and in compliance with our individual or personal center—whatever it is—so we can achieve and maintain stability. It is a demanding balancing act.

Is it any different from walking a tightrope? Whatever analogy we come up with, we understand, and are aware of the balancing feat that is so draining, exhilarating, and challenging, all at the same time. How do we not fall off? How do we regain our focal point as human emotions routinely fluctuate? How do we stay centered, balanced, stable, and effective?

Balance is what we need, what we long for, smooth sailing without banging from side to side or falling off and crashing. What is the secret? We know it is not remaining stagnate, but how do we successfully navigate within our boundary circles? We need to quickly regain equilibrium and maintain it to the place where all is well.

In the meantime, hang on!

chapter 6

CIRCLES-CYCLES-WHIRLWINDS

Life is compared and analyzed as movements in a cycle (i.e., dust to dust!). Seasons of life come and go, but they are not described as rectangles, squares, or any other geometric design but rather as circles, as orbital. Some terms we hear are circle of love or of influence; cycle of life, of pain; menstrual cycle, life cycles, product life cycles; etc. A circle or cycle is an interval of time during which an expected change or sequence occurs and eventually leads back to the starting point.

The circle is perfectly balanced, equal everywhere from its center (or core) to its boundary. If a circle maintains the same distance to its center, the same pressure, with no weakened areas, it is recognized as a "perfect circle." It is balanced. A circle has no vulnerable areas until we change its dynamics and cause imbalance.

When NASA revealed one of the images from its satellites, the earth appeared like an awesome perfect blue marble. I understand the solar system is not rotating in perfect circles but elliptically (in a closed-plane curve with a point moving in such a way that the sum of its distances from two fixed points is a constant). The focus is on the fixed constant. Amazingly, the earth appears as a perfect blue circle.

Commit to Change

How can we ever begin to understand the enormity of our universe and the discoveries unfolding at such a rapid pace? The common person does not comprehend the Milky Way, solar bursts, or light-years enough to engage in an intelligent conversation, let alone a debate. Yes, there are brilliant minds and geniuses that are amazed and enthralled with the reality of such dimensions, and do have the knowledge to understand, but most of it remains far beyond most inhabitants of this planet's grasp.

As overwhelming as it is, it is exciting and wonderful to behold and discover. What does the woman in a Third World nation think as she gazes into the atmosphere? What do poor or illiterate persons conceive in their minds about the mysteries of our solar system? For that matter, how often does it even enter any of our minds—traders on Wall Street, busy homemakers, executives running to and fro? May we all be astounded by the amazing facts and new revelations about our universe. However, what difference do such unfathomable mysteries make in our everyday thinking and activities? We may occasionally be struck with awe, but life and its responsibilities seem to quickly overtake our thoughts. Our focus returns to our immediate needs.

We may not understand the amazing balance that is needed to sustain life as we know it, but we do understand the need for a bicycle wheel to be in balance, or a vehicle's tires. Unbalanced wheels or tires cause uneven wear and tear on the product, as well as a bumpy ride. Life sure can have its bumps and bruises, causing one to wonder, *Okay, where am I off my path and out of my orbit?* I think we all have difficulties, with many troubling thoughts, highs and lows, and individual whirlwinds, all of which are part of the life cycle!

It may be scary when you do not understand or comprehend some things. It can leave you feeling inferior, skeptical, angry, and many other emotions. We want to understand, but it sometimes involves leaving behind some "truths" that we have believed and held onto for a long time. When change and new discoveries threaten our security, we need something to hold on to. We need an anchor. We do not want to spin out of control. A new arena may seem terrifying when everything we thought was true or right is being questioned, examined, and shaken. What is happening? Am I cracking up? What can I face and not face, see and refuse to see?

The more involved you are in searching and trying to grasp new ideas, the more you may discover things that were not previously evident, things you never wanted to know. It hurts to realize that systems or conclusions are flawed. Being hit with the frailties of humanity is an eye-opener. No matter how pure, innocent, or generous the original intent and the mission statement sounds, there are defects. Outcomes may be exaggerated or omitted, depending on what benefits the originator. The circle is not in balance; your sphere has been thrown into a rough ride. Is there a constant that is good and true?

What do we do with the new awareness that something is afoul in our midst when we have faithfully and eagerly supported and promoted an ideal or an organization? How do you not throw in the towel and give up the element of trust? It is like a divorce with betrayal that stings deeply. One wonders what to do next or where to go.

How do you avoid becoming irrational, critical, angry, or resentful? How do you embrace the valuable lessons learned to avoid the same pitfalls? What sustains hope? Do you leave? Do you remain? You know change is needed, but fear and intimidation are real obstacles.

These perplexing situations are difficult. You truly care about the concept and its potential, but some things are just not right. You voice your concerns, and many times, it works out wonderfully. Sometimes it will not. Are you willing to cut the ties and move on?

At times like these, we must get back in our orbit, rightly aligned with the center and in perfect rotation. It takes self-introspection and identity realignment. What is at your core? That is the only place that you will line up to go on, progress, mature into a better person, and complete your cycle.

I had a profound encounter at an amazing dance, and I would like to share it with you soon.

> Have the courage to say no. Have the courage to face the truth. Do the right thing because it is right. These are the magic keys to living your life with integrity.
>
> —Mark Twain, 1835–1910

chapter 7

INTRUSIVE EVENTS

As a woman who left home to travel with her military husband and have a family, I have experienced many challenges and pain that I have embraced but do not ever want to revisit. However, many exciting joys and wonders have also touched my life, which I love to recall and share with others.

Pains and trials are to be seasoned and shared with wisdom and timing, not as trophies but as milestones of growth and change. Life experiences, especially very difficult and heartbreaking ones, can help another soul to find its way to bloom and grow in the midst of life's obstacles, when the timing is right.

There are all kinds of tragedies, surprises, shattering events that invade your life. They burst forth on the scene in so many unexpected ways and change you forever. A difficulty suddenly hits you, deep inside, without warning or awareness, and rips you in ways you never knew that you could be torn.

There are concerns of how painful or fearful events in life will affect yourself and others. You may see the fear, the worry, and the concern in loved ones. That is hard. Some occurrences are lonely battles that only you can confront and attempt to maneuver through successfully.

Many suddenlies come and go in one's lifetime, but one seared my soul to the brink of horrors that I had never known. It was a very dark season. The comeback time was slow, deliberate, and painful, but produced strength that I would never trade. It opened my eyes to an understanding of who I am and who my strength is, in greater depth, and I learned how not to become or remain a permanently broken vessel.

Nothing should ever have that much influence over a person's identity, but sometimes we must be broken to be restored to wholeness. Actually, our concept of wholeness, what we think it is, may only be a breath away from failure.

There are many ways to deal with pain. We stuff, we bury, we ignore, we build fortresses around ourselves, we implode or explode, but how often do we use the pain to forge us into beautifully fashioned instruments of love and understanding? Besides, how could this even be a possibility?

I have seen many cry out in anger with closed fists and demand answers. Why me? Why now? Blaming themselves, others, or God. I have witnessed so many good people suffer, and I have seen some filled with peace, others full of fear and anger. I understand death and dying more than some and a great deal less than others. I have worked in the medical profession for years and have attended to many who recovered from illness and many who did not. Family dynamics are as varied as anyone could imagine; however, as unique as they are, they contain common threads.

We may be able to handle disease and its effects better than catastrophic traumas or injustices. Betrayal by our loved ones, our country, betrayals of ideals or authority, can leave wounds that may never heal. Look at our nation now, with so many military personnel committing suicide daily, violence, racial tensions, and shootings in places we never thought they would occur. There is out of control anger, mental illnesses, posttraumatic stress, and abuses of many kinds (e.g., rape, pedophilia, human trafficking, the conning out of one's life savings or identity). All are issues that tear at your soul, or at least they should. So how do we help one another? How do we help ourselves?

I am just one person. Time, energy, finances, ability, and even knowing or understanding what or how to help is often beyond comprehension and ability. The pain of the circumstances may get so overwhelming that one feels the weight of the injustice, and it will consume us if we do not figure out how to handle effectively.

No, we cannot ignore it. We cannot fix it. There are some things recommended to help: call, write, give, picket, demonstrate, confront, walk for a cause, pray, fast, unite, join an organization, start a group, and on and on. However, satisfaction does not come from just doing, by taking up a cause or doing what seems right to you. It is never enough, and the whirlwind blows. The body wearies, the mind battles, the zeal falters, and we must rest. We crave answers. We need solutions and long for peace. Oh, how do we get off this merry-go-round, because it is surely not the childhood fun ride?

Many do find a way to serve and help others through tragic loss or other injustices and thoroughly enjoy life. It does not appear as work but a privilege, a calling, a fulfillment, and what a powerful experience it is for the individual to help others. It produces purpose and contentment. They know they are where they are supposed to be, know their portion and handle it. They are prepared to help others come through rough waters, out of deep pits or any disparate heartbreaking circumstances, with hope for the future.

Seasons come and go, and so does direction and contentment. Change is good and is often a stepping-stone of growth. Many pitfalls try to entangle us in webs of deception and prevent satisfaction and destiny. So, how do we see, how do we recognize, how do we respond and productively advance?

The mind tends to run in circles, searching, seeking truth and solutions to produce the best outcome. Often the time is right for a pause. Take a deep breath, rest, and revisit it tomorrow like our famous Scarlet in *Gone with the Wind*.

The dawn will come, and we must continue our quest!

chapter 8

SUDDENLIES

Events happen that you are in no way prepared for or expecting. These are *suddenlies*. They can be amazingly wonderful surprises that astound and fill you with indescribable joy. Unfortunately, I have seen, heard, and experienced that far too many suddenlies are life-threatening, life-changing, devastating, shaking one to the very core of life's meaning. A tailspin with seemingly insurmountable obstacles may overwhelm and create doubt that life will never be the same.

Even when there is a warning of a horrific event, our minds may project it away from us, or it draws us into a shell for protection or denial.

The very word sudden suggests something happens unexpectedly, abruptly, or instantly. It breaks into our present and changes it immediately.

Even the idea of abrupt intervention in a life sounds frightful. However, several suddenlies delight me. I remember the Bible story of the announcement of a Savior's birth. Long ago, there were some shepherds in a field, perhaps milling around, resting, and talking among themselves, when an angel appeared to them. The glory of the Lord shone around them, and they were terrified.

> But the angel said to them, Do not be afraid, I bring you
> good news of great joy that will be for all the people. Today

in the town of David a Savior has been born to you: You will find a baby wrapped in cloths and lying in a manager.

—Luke 2:10–12, NIV

If that was not enough to shake them up:

Suddenly, a great company of the heavenly host appeared with the angel, praising God and proclaiming: Glory to God in the highest and on earth peace to men on whom his favor rests.

—Luke 2:13–14, NIV

That was a *wow* moment! Thankfully only one appeared first, or we might never have heard the rest of the story, as Paul Harvey used to say. For at the appearance of one, they were terrified. *Whew*, that is a sight hard to imagine! An angelic appearance in Scripture always seems to have been a suddenly with profound impact.

Nevertheless, in our everyday lives, what do we have to draw on or fall back upon if a suddenly happens? Consider the devastating tsunamis that have hit in the past few years. Even though there was some warning and some escaped, many could do nothing. Many were caught unaware and unprepared. Lives were forever changed. Nations were tragically affected. Our world shuddered and grieved. All too frequently, the invasions of life come in raging floods, fires, earthquakes, tornados, hurricanes—all acts of nature, hitting with force beyond our comprehension or our ability to stand in the path and not be affected, even if we are adequately prepared.

Tragically, sometimes it takes one of these astronomical events of nature to shake us out of complacency. In fact, when such tragedies hit, there is usually worldwide outpouring of compassion, help, assistance, and provision.

A personal devastating suddenly may go unnoticed by the world and perhaps even by those closest to you. They do not see, know, or understand, or they may turn away because they cannot face you. Often you remain in the pain, the disillusionment, the life-shattering event ... alone.

Such happenings leave you vulnerable and open to scrutiny and judgment, minimizing your event, your emotions, your *suddenly*! The rest of the world goes on as if nothing happened.

Nevertheless, there is good news, and we can be prepared. We will continue our quest for guidelines and answers to difficult situations and ways to navigate through them victoriously.

chapter 9

MOMENTS

What is a moment? As the saying goes, *it will be just a moment* or *I will be with you in a few minutes*. Oh my goodness, how it seems like eternity as a child, when told *just a minute, honey* and how frustrating as an adult waiting on a live person to finally come on your cell phone to address your inquiry.

I think we have watered down the meaning of moment. We live in such a fast-paced technological age that it is almost impossible to seize the moment. Our thoughts are continually bombarded with more information, more demands, more action. How do you recognize moments?

Webster's Dictionary defines moment as (1) a minute measure of time: instant (2a) present time, (2b) a time of excellence, (2c) importance in influence or effect-notable.

How many moments are we noting? Do we see the moment the sun breaks forth on the horizon or its last display before darkness? Do we notice the first star appearing in the night sky? We have thousands of encounters daily—the little child running, the older woman smiling as she walks by, the kind man who opens the door for you or helps you pick up a paper you dropped, an order served by a faithful server, a gentle breeze, and so much more. Do we take time to appreciate or even notice events and spectacular displays of nature's beauty, or do they silently pass by unnoticed, and do people all around us remain faceless?

Do we embrace the present moment and make it one of excellence, or do they all roll on and on in familiarity and obscurity in our busy schedules?

We have heard the phrases: *slow down, stop to smell the roses.* You cannot take it with you, so slow down. What does it take to awake to gifts in our moments? We catalog tragic moments—9/11, Hurricane Katrina or Sandy, the snowstorm of such and such a year, a death, other tragedies. When do we capture the beauty of life without pain or distractions?

Yes, we have pleasant memories—the first kiss, the thrill of a sporting event, an award, marriage, a spectacular achievement, the birth of a child—but eventually, the great moments become fading memories, tucked away or forgotten due to the pressures of life.

We are constantly remembering the past or ignoring it and focusing entirely on the future. Is it imperative to set a goal and have an agenda in order? Where do we pause in our present moments? When do we recognize excellence around us? Is it possible—yes, it is! It requires discipline. It requires change. It demands it if we want to live fully in the present. Well, more about that later. Need to run to some of my moment-snatching ways.

Be back soon.

◆━━━ *section 2* ━━━◆

A DEEPER LOOK

A person often meets his destiny on the road he took to avoid it.

—Jean de La Fontaine, 1621–1695

←——————————————→

chapter 10

THE CONTINUED WALK

In the battle to secure a sense of balance, pride often presents as "king of the mountain," demanding attention, success, and proof of it (boasting). Self-pity is another face or dimension that presents as a lowly worm, perceived as a "whiner," also with its demands to be noticed. It is perhaps the flipside of pride. One can try to get that worm in shape and walking upright with respect, and along comes a bystander, placing a robe around it and a crown on its slimy head, for pulling itself up. Oh, not again. The robe and crown are burdensome; they are discarded before "king pride" knocks them off.

The sheer joy of running full force without hindrances or thought is exhilarating. Oops, someone is wounded, hurting and obstructing the path. Pride chooses the pattern—this does not affect me. It (pride) will not become involved and ignores the situation and moves on unless there is obvious praise and recognition. Self-pity may whine and say, "I am nothing. I feel sorry for you, but I cannot help due to my own circumstances."

Nevertheless, sometimes an awakening comes and oh the pain of recognizing self-centeredness and the conviction of a wrong attitude. Quickly condemnation and guilt shout their ugly accusations. Swirling, swirling down again into pits of despair! Do not go. Cling to any shred of dirt you can get under your fingernails, or grab any root or substantial branch that can stop the downslide and use to pull yourself up out of the mire. One knows that is not where they want to be. Pride and self-pity must find a way to the right action or spiral deeper into darkness.

In what small way can someone be of assistance to one in need when they themselves are facing hardships and difficulties? What small act of kindness can one share or give? Notice them, accept them, reach out and acknowledge their presence, their needs, their desperation, even though you may not be able to meet a specific need. A real need for acknowledgment of existence and purpose has been met when one takes brief moments of time to listen and to reach out to others. You often find help in your own dilemmas as you help others.

Lend a hearing ear and a helping hand wherever you can and try to understand. Choose not to judge, do not give unsolicited advice or question how or why they are in their current mess (at least, this is what most of us would appreciate). This could be any of us and perhaps was in another time, not exactly the same but in essence, the same struggles, pain, and woundedness. Reality and responsibility confront everyone.

Since it is obvious that no one has all the answers or provisions they need, someone might need to direct them to another source, someone who is trustworthy and capable in the particular situation, or who can further lead them to needed resources. Nevertheless, do not ignore them or pass them by. Your season of denial or ignoring has been shaken to bring you back to purpose and balance.

So the search for truth and understanding continues, not just for myself but also in the hope that together we may run, laugh, and enjoy life. Sometimes go at a snail's pace to reflect on life, enjoy the beauty, and stop to smell the roses. What a privilege it is getting to know one another, all the while expanding our circle of life and influence as we grow in the process.

chapter 11

ENTITLEMENT

Sometimes thinking we deserve something, or that something is our right, is a horrible snare. It can be very deceptive and even disrespectful. We can have so many circles of expectations that they become entangled like a Chinese puzzle. So much can be taken for granted that we harden our hearts to gratefulness and move into the "bubble of entitlement."

As we mentally lay claim to a position, an inheritance, a gift, we have opened our self up to disappointment and disillusionment regardless of how subtle our expectations seem. We have positioned our self in a place of authority, but one that is dependent on the action of another, the one who holds the access key to "our entitlement."

When the other person becomes aware of your preconceived ideas and timing, many feelings can result. Some of the common reactions are feelings of being taken advantage of, or of being taken for granted, of anger, of *How could you?* Perhaps, you will receive what you are expecting and waiting for but your timing is out of sync with the benefactor. Thereby, you have overstepped your boundaries and have dishonored the one in the position to grant the gift.

So many times, excitement pushes us past restraint, lust creates a hunger not to be easily satisfied, and greed overrules acceptable control or thought. Fear may drive the need for a *now* answer or solutions, just in case the supply dwindles or is depleted. We are not able to take back our words or actions, and our reputation is hanging midair after we have wounded or insulted another. Now, where will the gavel fall?

One may turn on charm, tears, or even angry threats to receive their perceived entitlement. Patience and trust are dismissed, and determination to rule their personal world and obtain what they want in the desired timeframe is the looming goal. The real motive is often cloaked in deception, flattery, hyped-up needs, or feigned appreciation. This mask needs to be ripped off. Consider, do you need "mask removal" in any area of your life?

We know that it is best not to be impatient and try to manipulate circumstances, but it is difficult to wait. Patience is a virtue, as the saying goes, with gratitude and thankfulness being close cousins.

However, sometimes we are denied or wrongfully not given something that is rightfully ours. This is painful, and other life lessons must be learned. Nonetheless, many practice the self-declaration of entitlement; it is a trap. It robs many of self-respect, respect of others, dependence, false hopes, and the list goes on. There is a better way.

Is it not better to walk in confidence and assurance that all your needs will be met and that you have a good future ahead? Again, we will look at that life-changing choice shortly.

> Don't go around saying, the world owes you a living. The world owes you nothing. It was here first.

—Mark Twain, 1835–1910

chapter 12

DEATH-TAXES-DECISIONS

We have heard it said that no one escapes death or taxes, two realities that adults face. However, sometimes we wish it were that simple, as hard as that may be! Choices and decisions crowd our minds every second of life. Therefore, for now, we will not make a decision. We will wait and address the issue later. Wow, a choice made, a decision cast.

Every thought, action, deed, is a choice, a decision. Some actions are so automatic and routine that we are not even aware of them; we just function. Nevertheless, we all face crossroads of impact, choices, decisions, that alter our lives, the lives of others, our futures, or our circumstances. Real-life issues are at times mindboggling and taxing. Some struggle more than others do in forming or completing decisive actions. Some engage in deep research, some throw the dice, so to speak, some agonize; others choose to ignore and postpone the final conclusion as long as possible. Regardless, all choices are decisions set in motion.

It seems once again that life's motion can be cyclic or circular, not always linear. We often face the same challenges over and over again, just in different wrappers. We have honed our skills or coping methods and our analytical tactics, but they seem to go back repeatedly to basics. The core of our being seeks a deeper and purer method to pursue the "right way." What is it?

It is as if there is an inside monitor, an innate knowing sometimes. A new idea presents with an uncertain road, and there is a pause, a question, a gnawing inside. Then the mind accelerates to supersonic speed. I must research this. I must know because it does not sit right with me. Alternatively, do not be foolish. Do not rock the boat and just stay aboard.

No, one must do diligence and be responsible. Self-improvement books, classes, and seminars offer answers. One must be knowledgeable. Self-improvement is critical and may support self-interest, awareness, and eventually promotion. The top of the game is paramount; understanding this new phenomenon with exciting insights and concepts enables you to remain in the power game of knowledge, recognition, and advancement.

However, something within lingers. What is this nagging sensation? It is not right. Well, how could it not be right? Look at who and how many are in support of this ideal. What is wrong with me? It has to be me. Oh my, it seems like everything always shifts back to me. Why am I different? Why I am struggling? Oh, dear, it is all about me, just in a different shroud! I must go on. I must fit in. I must understand. I must know, or the alternative is I am less, I am defective. Oh no, spiraling into defeat is not an option. The pressure is on. Am I the only one who sees the risk or flaws in the presented plan?

Again, as you try to balance the pendulum from one viewpoint to another, you often sense that familiar call to relax and to wait. There is truth found within. Even as deceptive and distorted as views can become, there is a thing we call conscience. It reveals truth if we do not override it in our haste to move on up or to fit in. It gives no peace to be agreeable or compromise for only the purpose to lower a threat or enhance possibilities. The "something" inside seeks to be acknowledged.

It is hard to stand alone. Because there is also that persistent nagging fear that you may be wrong. We know we have been wrong before. So what is different now?

It is settled, I cannot agree that this issue, concern, decision, teaching, is right for me. I cannot. I will die inside if I yield to the pressure. I do not need to picket, to attack, to present my view as best or right, but I cannot ignore my convictions. I must continue to wait and live life with the truths that I believe I have within.

Change is real, and I must remain open to change, but it needs to align with individual values. Others' views matter, and I will treat my neighbor as I hope to be treated. Do I attempt to engage in dialogue? Is confrontation the answer? Can understanding and acceptance appear? Risk is inevitable but often worthwhile.

Let us agree to address later. When a personal foundation is violently shaken, it is very challenging to redefine beliefs without destroying oneself. Freedom and peace are the desired goal. Often answers come as we wait and trust that we are protected and led in truth.

Join the waiting game!

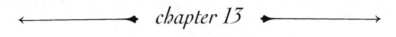

chapter 13
REPUTATION

So much is wrong with the saying "Sticks and stones may break my bones, but words will never hurt me." What a lie!

Maybe we should heed the words of an Indian philosopher and teacher.

> Whatever words we utter should be chosen with care for people will hear them and be influenced by them for good or ill.

—Gautama Buddha, 563–483 BCE

I have experienced broken bones, joints, and painful words. The words cut deeper. The healing takes longer. Words cut at your moral fiber, your identity. They may attack your mind day and night. The battle is wearying. Do I minimize physical pain, by no means, but I know the pain of words and actions. The physical body often heals quicker; the soul shrinks back in fear of non-value. Verbal and physical insults and assaults both try to suck life out of you and demoralize you into a nothing. The enemy tries to control you completely, whether in your home, at your place of employment, or in social circles.

When someone you love hurts you deeply, it is devastating. Words fueled by lies spoken by one you trust, who knows you and your heart and yet speaks callously against your character, may possibly be fueled by insecurity or anger. Others hear. It feeds and fuels a fire that is never quenched. You can forgive, you can move on, but something has been stolen, and it will never be the same. The attack is often coupled, both physically and verbally.

Some brush it off, some ignore it, and some try to explain it away by excusing it as drama or as exaggeration, all the while leaving you wounded and face down in the dirt with their foot on your neck. Yes, they have gone on, taken their boot and words with them, but you know the depth of the attack. They may even feel righteous and justified in their expression and actions.

What are you to do after a wrong and injurious accusation? To explain or justify the scene, the perpetrator may have convened a roundtable of listeners and informed them before you ever knew this was going on. Oh, yes, great minds have a consensus now. You are examined, accused, and judged and are now expected to go on with life. Your perspective has been deciphered and conscience eased without any input from the one being dissected. Gossip has blossomed, judgments made, and you feel isolated and alone. Information was shared far beyond where it should have gone. Many do not want to get further involved or hear any more, and you are again wounded. Do not do this to one another. Talk first with the person that you have a question for and need to verify a position or statement. Do not hear it secondhand then thirdhand and then roundtable, with conclusions already established.

chapter 14

STOP THE DOWNLOAD!

*Wise men speak because they have something to say;
fools because they have to say something.*

—Plato, 429–347 BCE

Whether you are the one hearing or sharing the grand conclusion or the one wronged, it is a painful situation. The one betrayed is abandoned, and lip-service platitudes may follow, but often rifts never heal, and a reputation is ruined. The very word *reputation* means your overall quality or character judged by others. When an assessment is ruthless, one's reputation will never be the same, and unfortunately, few ever say they are sorry. A life, a soul, crushed.

An uphill battle must be fought to escape the pit where you have been thrown and brutally discarded. To emerge whole and beautiful is a miraculous undertaking where focus, effort, and hope should all culminate.

Where do you go? What do you do? Regardless which side of the scenario you lie (talking about someone or the one being scrutinized), should never be considered acceptable behavior. Please stop.

May we all gain wisdom that will lead us into true caring about one another.

chapter 15

IDENTITY STRUGGLES

So much energy is expended as one tries desperately to be what they think they should be; the risk looms that there will be nothing left of me. The battle rages to be a good little girl or boy, to please everyone, to stay clean, and to say and do the exact right thing. Where is the joy of spontaneity and creativity? I have heard many stories about cute antics, how alive and active I was, how ornery. However, not everyone appreciates high energy and cuteness, and love and acceptance was sometimes overshadowed by negative words that were slowly replacing concepts of acceptance. Negative comments drowned out positive assessments, and lies were believed as truth. Insecurity and rejection had too much influence in my personal life for far too long. Many like me struggled and still struggle to remain on the "perfect path" to happiness.

There were many laughs, many fun and happy times, but inside, there were raw, gaping holes from so many comparisons, lies, and failures. I had a wonderful family, full of flaws but a good family. I was by most standards—smart, active, excelling at school and making many friends, but at the same time, there was a gnawing inside, seeking completion. To many, my life might have appeared near perfect—not rich, not poor, just in the middle. Others might think I was a millionaire or a pauper. Perspective is such a strange phenomenon.

However, this is not about the details, the words, or the circumstances that provided an often-visited place just to say it existed. As I grew, the baggage of insecurity, rejection, and a bubbly personality, full of hope and energy, were all vying to fit inside me and battling for space and supremacy.

I married. Wow, a completely new arena of love, of emotions and experiences so fresh, alive, and amazing to me. Joy jumped to the forefront. Excitement was winning the battle, but soon, the unworthiness, the insecurity, and the rejection would rear their ugly heads. Oh, but their stays would be short. I was so in love and loved the ability to give, to receive, and to embrace the marriage union of oneness.

I was still on the trajectory of perfection, yet it grew more difficult as time marched on. Moves, changes, and additions came, our first-born entered our realm. What an explosion of joy, wonder, and, oops, insecurity. How was I to be perfect? Work, little sleep, and more responsibilities ensued, but the beauty of the nucleus of family was worth it all.

I was balancing the act fairly well even with relocation after relocation due to career. Amazing joy number two, three, and four arrived within a few years. There were many blessings of such joy, hope, anticipation, and yet fear loomed in the background. How can one stretch the energy and stay on top of the row? It was getting harder, and the wonderful changes had many hidden and unexpected challenges. I was hungry for and needed answers. I needed more assistance, more strength, more patience, and more love. As I soaked up learning, reading, and praying, I would be filled, but there were so many claims on my resources that I was like a barrel shot full of holes, and I continually leaked out the fullness. I was young, still in my twenties.

I had to be strong. I needed to remain creative, happy, loving, patient, and balanced, all while providing for the family. I had to be strong, perfect! I was driven to make the best of every situation. A good parent provides all that is needed for the precious family, a knightess in shining armor. I was so blessed, yet I was drowning. No one noticed. The mask was good. When did worry overtake joy and exhaustion diminish life's fullness? Fear also tried to overtake the thrills and dread to squelch the joy.

The struggles did not stop with immediate family needs. Oh no, parents, siblings, extended family, friends, and acquaintances, many experiencing personal tragedies and crises. Nations at war, regimes crumbling, fear, hunger, human trafficking, abuses of all kinds, soldiers critically wounded with life-changing challenges ahead, all whirling thoughts that demanded awareness and attention. I was losing my identity and trying to balance an act that I was unable to do alone. I could not carry the weight of the pain and injustices in the world.

Focus regains perspective. What is perspective? How do you grasp the horrors of life and not be affected and changed? Do you deny, do you bury your emotions or your head in the sand? Do you puddle-jump from one circle of awareness or crises to the next? How does one equalize or weigh options, time, and focus? How do you sustain the ideal of perfection? How is one not to deny circumstances, not to simplify, not to overload, and above all, not to ignore? It is an ongoing choice to remain hopeful and full of joy amid tragic realities and endless responsibilities and learn from heartache and unmerited blessings.

The battle for discovering and embracing identity is not limited by age or gender. All must search for their unique qualities and paths in life's journey. No one is more important or less valuable than another. We need "special hearts" (tender and teachable) to understand the internal strivings and to embrace the true self and identity that each has been created to discover. It is critical to reclaim your innate identity, free from self and other's expectations.

There is a glimmer of light and truth within that cries out for freedom, peace, an unseen call, and hope. The temptation to fall back into old habits and ways of doing and thinking are present, but you recognize it and can now choose to deny it, and with a spring in your step, you leave the old baggage behind.

Hear the call of the dance. Oh what a ballroom, an awakening dance, your Partner is beckoning!

chapter 16

NARROW MINDED OR NARROW PATH?

The ironies of life can become so convoluted and intertwined. We strive to figure things out, but with so many perpetual changes in values, opinions, and insights, all integral parts of the mysteries of the life cycle, it is a continuous endeavor.

It is amazing the advancement in the fields of industry, technology, medicine, environment, transportation, health, and many more arenas that occur in one's lifetime, let alone since the beginning of time. Daily activities are easier with these advancements, but what is foundational for societies to be productive, healthy, prosperous, and in accord?

View a minute-long segment of any newscast, and you witness the discord in the world. It flashes its divisive head in all arenas—race, economy, gender, traditional marriage and variations of family structure, right to choose, right to life, creation, evolution, education, politics, and religion. On and on goes the repetitive cycle of discussion, accusation, blame, and judgment, resulting in massive, seemingly impenetrable barriers. We long to communicate and to see issues resolve, but we want our own way: "the right way"!

Webster's Collegiate Dictionary states, "right: to lead straight, direct rule, righteous, being in accordance with what is just, good or proper, correct, and an agreeable standard conforming to truth."

Truth, oh my. Everyone thinks they have the truth or the true way to lead to happiness or to solve a situation. How do we ever come to the realization of truth and walk together in harmony?

There has to be some acceptable standard. I do not believe that it can be everyone doing what they feel is right. I cannot accept human trafficking, sexual, physical, emotional abuse, or bondage, or driving at whatever speed one determines they feel like, whether they are under the influence of drugs or alcohol or just in a hurry.

What does Webster have to say about wrong? "Injurious unfair or unjust act action or conduct inflicting harm-immoral unethical contrary to goodness equity or law." It is also "not according to moral standards improper to truth, without regard for what is proper."

Again, we come to the crossroads of what each considers right, wrong, acceptable, and proper.

I do not believe or practice many things due to personal moral values. This very fact places me in a category that some label as archaic, narrow-minded or ignorant. This is unfair judgment, and I know very well that it swings both ways, many ways.

Nevertheless, I do know that once my standard of values is accepted within, I must adhere to them until I see where I have misunderstood the standard. Until then, I aim to be considerate, kind, and respectful to others, not abasing anyone. I believe we are all created by One God and uniquely positioned for a relationship with Him and our destiny.

Therefore, if I do not adhere to another's opinion or standard of right or wrong, it does not make me narrow-minded. I am trying to remain on the narrow path set before me and proceed in joy with love, compassion and wisdom, and in freedom from judging others and myself. It is a difficult path, steep and with many pitfalls, precipices, and or edges, which might delay or change my viewpoint. It is an arduous climb—very lonely at times, very demanding, but also full of such beauty and peace that can envelop you in a moment. You know that you have chosen right. A Presence within provides contentment amid much turmoil. The circumstances no longer matter; you are true to yourself and without putting anyone down.

How do you respond to those in your midst whose views drastically oppose your views and values? Do you surround yourself with those who hold the same beliefs and taunt the opposition identified as the enemy? Do you try to shame, humiliate, and expose their faults or just outshout them?

I ponder how to be the best me and honor my Creator and Restorer. I must try to stay on the narrow path set before me, judge no one and belittle no one. I strive to be all I can be and honor the One who called me to my destiny. I have friends of many colors, of many intellectual and economic levels, of different lifestyle choices, of those who have fallen into very desperate straits and those who have phenomenally great successes. I identify with each. I hurt when they hurt. I rejoice when they rejoice. I care. I am comfortable in their presence.

I did not come to this place easily or alone. I have been in the school of the Spirit for years with major correction, adjustment, and discipline. It is very painful at times, yet work and change continue. The joy of success in the change to deeper love with nonjudging attitudes is beyond comprehension, and so it is worth all the painful awareness of my inadequate attempts at doing and being right while seeking greater understanding and depth.

The training is ongoing, and it may never end. I choose a trainable heart, and I am ecstatic with my Teacher. He is faithful and true.

chapter 17

MISUNDERSTOOD OR GUILTY

Oh my, the pitfalls, twists, and turns of life keep one twirling. Sometimes innocence or guilt does not matter. The path to healing is the same cry from within. Help!

Mistakes may have high consequences to pay. Many have been victimized; however, we all make mistakes; some search for the path to wholeness, while others continue their descent into darkness.

There is a deep cry within that this is not where we want to be or how it is meant to be. How do we change, regardless of life's circumstances, the cards that we have been dealt?

In spite of how perfect and fulfilling one's life may be, we all experience disappointments and painful situations. It is our responsibility to seek and find the answer. How do we become a better person through difficult times?

I have jumped around with many examples and situations that may we face in life but skirted what I believed to be the answer. Who is the answer?

Previously, I stated that I have had much pain and grief in my life, but compared to some, my life was a bowl of cherries (sweet, delicious morsels of delight—with pits). Regardless of the hand dealt, we all have common ground. I believe we have a Creator Father who longs to hold us, a perfect Father who has extended open arms, heart, ears, and love to all. Regardless of our past, present, or future, He longs that all of us know Him.

Some may be angered or skeptical at this statement, but if even one has decided to continue identifying with me, perhaps the hunger for answers is genuine. I cannot convince anyone, but I do know what I have faced in my life, and I know the joy of His arms and the amazing plan that unfolds as I lean into His realm and seek to understand and know Him more.

This is what I can offer. The joy of learning to lay it all down, to ask for and receive love and understanding from One who knows everything about me. Everything!

I want someone, "The One" who does not expose me, abuse me, or turn me away. Many ask, then why did He allow such and such to happen? Ask Him. Let Him walk the path with you and reveal where He was and is and what He has done and is in the process of doing. Spend time alone with Him. Be patient. Lay down your anger and any preconceived ideas, and seek truth. Wait for insight and answers instead of demanding them. However, not every question is answered in one's lifetime, but if you get to know Him intimately, you can release the matter to Him as His love and peace fill and assure you of His goodness.

I want Him to share my life's journey, my struggles, and teach me His ways of dealing with pain and disappointments and how to embrace hope, joy, and security. I really do not know how to simply share with you. God, who is so powerful, loving, and amazing, has relentlessly pursued me and changed my life and destiny.

He reveals such splendor that is beyond comprehension and yet speaks of tiny insignificant matters that can blow me away. His kindness is so full of love and mercy, it astounds me and makes me feel like a safe and cherished humble woman. It is overwhelming love. I cannot absorb it all, but every fiber of my being feels love and acceptance. I want to remain in that place, but it is yet to be permanent. There is work to be accomplished in the here and now. I must receive His instruction in the moments and be strengthened and encouraged to go forth.

Thank you for hanging with me. An open crack in the exterior of my sharing has emerged. Perhaps more will surface later. I have some very personal dreams that I would like to share.

chapter 18

CRUSHED IN THE MIDDLE

How do you stand, how do you breathe, where is the rest, where is the peace, when you know two loved ones are broken and experiencing deep pain? The spillover splashes onto other loved ones. How do you stop the accusations, the judgments, the opinions, and the dividing walls from going higher and higher?

The pain is deep as you see two with gaping wounds, wondering, *Why, why, why?* Betrayal is ugly. A deep, searing pain that drags you further and further down affects you more and more. What comfort is there? What answers are there? What do you say? Do you disown, reject, hate? How can they forgive one another? How do I forgive? How do others forgive? How does life go on with the knowledge that it will never be the same? Betrayal is raw pain.

I know from personal experience that it may take years to recover, and there are many steps to overcoming its many ramifications. Grief, shock, pain, hate, anger, rejection, and fears all pierce your soul. So many emotions rise up in critical junctions of life. Betrayal is one of those critical intersections. Betrayal can take many forms, but when it comes from those in your inner circle, closest to you, it cuts and wounds deeply. The effect may linger for a long time.

However, I have witnessed amazing results by some who were sickened by their act of betrayal and the consequences of it, and I have watched them overcome pain, guilt, shame, anger, excuses, and blame and become a better and stronger person. They were able to seek forgiveness and forgive themselves.

How does one respond to the one betrayed but also to the offender? Both are so fragile; both need help. Someone well trained to deal with the thoughts, feelings, fears, and all the emotions that flare up is a critical asset. Will they go? Will they open up and hear, share, receive? You hope and cry out for one who is compassionate, knowledgeable, and truthful, wrapped in love to lead them forward into healing.

It is one thing to experience betrayal, but to know and love both the parties involved is a very difficult place to be. How do you not add to their embarrassment, shame, guilt, or blame but only offer nonjudgmental support without appearing to condone the action? Remember never to engage in gossip—it helps no one. How do you comfort and share the horror of the offense without cutting anyone off?

Personally, your head may be spinning, your heart breaking, and your stomach churning. Tears dry up, and your call for help for those in their brokenness is ongoing. Hope arises, and a need to be still and to rest is evident.

If only someone could take it from them and carry the load. Or roll back the time and change the circumstances to prevent it from ever occurring. Someone needs to tell them the truth; they can heal and become a stronger person. They will need to address the negatives, grow in wisdom, and forgive, not be destroyed by destructive thought patterns. This process is a fierce battle. Growth and change burst forth when acknowledgment, open communication, responsibility, and forgiveness are embraced. Others affirm their love and support, but a veil of secrecy and judgment may remain and usually delays healing. When and where is the door of healing and restoration?

When such situations hit close to my heart, I need to seek the One who does understand and holds the answers. I know I need to meet with God. He alone can mend the broken vessels. I am thankful, and I pray that the process will be gentle, full of grace, mercy, and restoration. May powerful changed lives come forth and face life with strength, wisdom, and understanding.

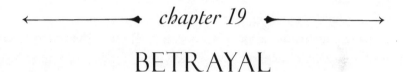

chapter 19

BETRAYAL

In the previous chapter, I briefly mentioned betrayal as one of those horrors that interrupts your life suddenly. To spotlight betrayal is to retrieve or summon painful memories. As a child we experience the feelings of betrayal when a friend does not ask us to sit with them, or when you see two friends walking away laughing and overhear their hurtful remarks about you or others, mocking and making fun because of attire, not making the team, etc. The sting is real; the pain is real. You grow, you adjust, you adapt, sometimes in ways that are not so helpful or healthy.

As life goes on, this enemy returns with greater depth, pain, and vengeance, with personal intent to harm and with the outcome to kill or severely wound areas deep within. The barb is sharper. The shame and pain nearly destroy you. You can no longer run to Mommy or Daddy and have them kiss you and tell you everything is all right when the ones closest to you, your most trusted allies, are the ones who have betrayed you. You are an adult now and expected to handle life's blows and protect yourself and your family.

What a load, and what did we learn from past hurts? Did we close ourselves off, build walls, and vow never to trust anyone again or allow access to our inner being? Did we lock the doors of our hearts and throw away the key? After someone has shredded your heart and stomped on the pieces, it seems as if these plans are viable and have self-preservation in focus. Is forgiveness possible? Is it feasible to recover from betrayal whole, better, and able to go on?

The very word—betray—is frightening. According to *Webster's Dictionary*, betray means "to lead astray (deceive), to deliver to an enemy, to fail or desert in time of need, to violate confidence, to prove false."

A betrayer often sets aside previous beliefs, promises, or values to gain what he or she desires. As in adultery, vows have been broken and hopes shattered. Angry words and accusations can be vicious and strike like a venomous snake, wounding deeply, to cover or protect oneself.

Defense takes many paths. Some more harmful than the betrayal itself. Walls of excuse, of blame, of defense, may grow higher and higher. Lies, truth, and memories haunt and taunt; the enemy is out to destroy all forms of life's best. Where is the path to freedom?

It is no longer little girls or boys' fickle ways. How deep, how far, will the damage go? How do we stop the downward spiraling? How does one come forth whole and free?

The battle is fierce. How do you stop paranoia? How do you discern truth? How do you choose to forgive and not hate or seek revenge? How do you hold your tongue and not openly share because you are trying desperately to stop the wildfire even though another lit the match? Yet, you know you need counsel and truth to see you through the ordeal to a healthy outcome.

The imagination rages, questions abound, blame screams for attention, pain courses throughout your entire being. Loneliness is almost overwhelming, but a time of withdrawal is necessary. Unfairness wants its day in court. A wounded spirit is left to wonder what happened? Why? What is wrong with me?

So how does one go on? We cannot even see to pick up the pieces—whether over infidelity, gossip, abuse, accusations, lack of promotion or recognition. Betrayal takes many forms, and so does the reaction to the offense.

Some stuff emotions and say, "Get on with life." This may work for a while, but it will resurface. One may become cynical, bitter, judgmental, prideful, or insecure, and again, the choices, attitudes, and behavior are cyclical. Others may say it is like water off a duck's back; it will not stick;

just let it roll off, ignoring it while pretending it does not matter or hurt. When we do not successfully maneuver through hurts, we risk shallowness and detachment, using things and people only for personal needs or gain through control and manipulation to protect and satisfy ourselves.

Somewhere deep within the perpetrator or victim, he or she knows that some things will never be the same again. The grief and loss add to the crushing weight. The battle rages and is wearying.

However, there is hope that it is possible to come out of this nightmare changed, wiser, and stronger. Where is the revelatory path to freedom?

I have never needed peace, hope, reflection, or intimacy as deeply as when I have been betrayed or have betrayed another. I need the one and only Faithful One, who will never betray anyone. I want you to meet Him. I hope that you will consider His Goodness. Introductions are joyfully available and extended.

We should consider visiting the dance.

◆— *section 3* —◆

ROADS TRAVELED

*Life is a continuous adjustment of internal relations
to external relations.*

—Herbert Spencer, 1820–1903

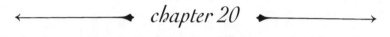

chapter 20

TRUST

Trust is such a powerful word and an elusive ability; it challenges understanding and reasoning. We trust in part by relying on experiences and attach the assessment to a concept taught and promoted, but it still may defy our grasp fully. Yes, we sometimes trust in things and people without even being aware, as will this bridge sustain the weight of the vehicle, a chair hold up our mass, instincts ensure a person is safe and good—in our parental guidelines, religious teachings, or patriotic values.

Yet, as we grow, learn, and hear different perspectives, questions arise.

We recognize that not everyone shares the same viewpoint, and your personal guidelines or boundaries may be under scrutiny. When your value system is exposed and not accepted, fear looms under the surface, warnings linger, predetermined ideals may shatter, and trust is challenged. It hurts. Doubt, criticism, anger, and other negative emotions may arise when mistrust challenges trust. It can be a shattering of the inner soul, clouding our thinking. Unchecked, it will paralyze our rational thinking.

According to *Webster's New Collegiate Dictionary*, trust is "assured reliance on the character, ability, strength, or truth of someone or something."

Confidence in character—of goodness, truth, and strength—is the expected reliability and foundation of the trust relation without fear of disappointment, harm, or deception. Trust goes deep within, and its shattering is a very painful experience.

Once your realm of trust has been broken, how do you rebuild it? How do you hope again? How do you balance expectations without fear of an undesirable outcome? Innocence has been stolen. How do you heal? How do you grow? How do you prepare yourself for future growth in conjunction with understanding and awareness?

Whom do you trust to help? Are you all alone? Who hears and understands your cries for help? Battles rage within: trust versus mistrust, truth versus lies, transparency versus deception, and faith versus fact.

Facts are not always the same as truth. Some are true but not the same. How do we separate? How do we comprehend truth and know what is trustworthy is a vital endeavor, a quest worthy of effort.

Can anyone see through the smokescreen? Can anyone blow the smoke away? Will one ever trust again? Will the heart beat to the rhythm of trust and assurance and not to the beat of fear, doubt, and skepticism?

Please, someone, hear the cry. Is anyone there? Does anyone care? Shattered, one cannot pick up the pieces. Will there ever again be wholeness?

I have heard of a place of healing. May we journey on in search of wholeness.

chapter 21

CONTINUING ON THE PATH BEFORE ME

How does one advance on this narrow path without offense? How does it make a difference? How do you help and share another's load as they travel on their journey?

When I was a little girl, my mother told me that I would not have a party unless everyone in the class was invited and that no presents were to be brought. I did not want any left out, especially if they could not afford to purchase something. I identified with the underdog from a very young age. However, this can lead you down such a path of empathy that you hurt along with the rest of the world, leaving little room for joy or hope.

It is difficult not to be swallowed up by all the pain and heartache, but one needs to remain in hope because there are many sunny days and much to be thankful for. We need to shift our gaze. When human tragedy strikes in nations far away, my heart would break, and I would try to be faithful to send what I could, hopefully for several months. It was difficult. Depression would try to rule because I did not know how to help more and felt ineffective and overwhelmed at times. Years have passed, and I unfortunately still experience that feeling of helplessness at times. But I know the Fount of All Provision, and I run for the refreshing drink.

I hear and see organizations raising money for the victims of overwhelming tragedies. Actors, musicians, wealthy, and famous individuals perform live concerts or outreaches to aid the affected people and areas. One's heart swells with thanksgiving and appreciation. However, it hurts when you see these very same ones curse our land, our leaders, or those of different views. Why must we put one another down in an attempt to appear better than others? I do not believe this will ever be the path to wholeness or the healing of our nations or interpersonal relationships. We need to extend grace to all, regardless of their shortcomings or different views.

Many do not have the means, a platform, a voice, or the finances to express themselves noticeably, but their heart and expression of love and caring are a vital balance in our world. Each life matters, each prayer heard, each gift noticed by the One above us all.

So what does this grandmother have to say? How can she help now? Physical strength is definitely diminished but still available for appointed interventions. Even though my circle of life is coming back to its beginning—dust—there are still opportunities available to be helpful and effective in life. I want to make the best of every opportunity He provides for me to be used for His kingdom's purposes. I am so thankful for a God-provided Counselor.

The battle to focus on the narrow path and not cry out prejudice or point a finger of blame but forgive instead of keeping score—love and accept instead of hate and division—are real battle choices. How could anyone believe this is an easy choice? Dying to my own agenda, trying to hear and respect others' opinions, even while receiving jabs, judgments, and denials. I chose to continue onward with my head held high and my shoulders back, taking life in stride with humility and my heart bowed. It is hard, very hard! Oh, the many times I have failed, but I desire to remain on the path before me. The rewards are out of this world!

Can we walk together? No easy task when each is struggling so hard on his or her own path. After years of challenges and difficulties, I do recognize more easily the path not to take, and I settle joyfully in my narrow path and systematically proceed onward. I long to take your hand and proceed together.

The celebration and ecstasy when we do share a path successfully is so rewarding. May we walk together with respect, kindness, love, and hope and leave behind the barriers!

Our journey may have many detours, U-turns, failures, and falls. However, may we proceed on the path set before us with greater understanding and illumination. In addition, with the wisdom that the wide path well-traveled, though temporarily filled with shallow fun, is not the fulfillment for which one longs. It spirals out of control and destroys many unless the course is altered. The narrow path is never easy but becomes more intimate with inner joy, increasing trust and hidden rewards.

So many bubbles of ideology have popped or floated away. So many circles of friends, acquaintances, and family members are gone, some fading from memory and influence. Yet what remains is worth holding on to.

A vital tool to learn from is recall. Nothing in life replaces the power of personal experience and learned lessons. Careful assessment of what should be retained and what should be released is a crucial lesson of life. Cry out for wisdom and truth—may they be strong anchors in our journeys.

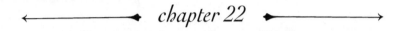

chapter 22

PERIODS OF UNREST

Have you ever felt all alone despite being surrounded by people? Turmoil is all around, and fear and anxiety interact. You sense pressure and high demands physically, mentally, and emotionally, and yet no one seems to notice your dilemma.

Happenings are frightening. The atmosphere is charged, swirling with what-ifs and unknowns. Yet the purpose of the time together with others demands attention. You desperately long to be with those of like minds and values, to share the burdens of the moments, but you must see this time through alone.

The air itself seems heavy. Oppression is threatening. The weight of so much evil, deception, and hopelessness is mounting. How is it so trivial to others? The prevailing attitude is ho-hum, let us stop for a while, take a break, take a walk, shop, eat, or find the nearest drink. As some find their remedy or escape, laughter swells, alcohol has its effects, and the joy of yet another purchase temporarily soothes the soul.

I walk, I think, I need to consider my thoughts. I need time to meditate, to cry out for understanding. I long to go to the dance, to read, and to be comforted, but the heaviness does not lift immediately. The secret "alone time" must wait. When I feel like I can wait no longer for solace, I recall (if not immediately visible) the beauty of a landscape, fields filled with sheep or cattle, the sky, the clouds, or mists of rain. Fresh air calms me, and the beauty of creation fills me and bring drops of mercy and hope that soothe my soul.

The awareness of how darkness can and does invade situations is very real. How blind we are to the reality of the battle. One longs to cry out about deep joy and revelation, yet is restrained. It is not time. We long for relief and inner peace, and we struggle with a lack of connectedness. I do not belong. We mingle and are polite, but there is a chasm. Raw fear—of how dark and lonely it may be in the future—rears its ugly head.

Horrors of the past and present are related and repeated. Something is trying to steal and destroy faith and hope. It cannot, but pressure and sadness are heavy. How long before the personal breakthrough? Quality personal time is so limited, and the body is truly weak. Many are weary, sick, and riddled with grumbling and complaining. We need rejuvenation. Bodies and souls wracked with pain and fatigue, but we will not let go. We cannot.

Brief encounters with hope come at junctions and at unexpected times or places. An appointment is made by One who knows all and orchestrates connections. Wow, you recognize the fresh wind, and you breathe it in and are thankful. You know you will complete the journey with the Master overseeing.

> Life is a shipwreck, but we must not forget to sing in the lifeboat
>
> —Voltaire, 1694–1778

When there is a time for reflection, you are able to see and understand more. Then a message comes, a reminder:

> But the Lord is faithful, and He will strengthen and protect you from the evil one.
>
> —2 Thessalonians 3:3, NIV

The floodgate opens with fresh springs, and the Word covers, washes, refreshes, and sustains you.

Why do these droughts and periods of deep testing come? Purifying motives, strengthening convictions, and deeper understanding are precious fruits when the clouds part and the pruning is temporarily halted. Secure and hide your treasures in your "treasure chest" and view the precious nuggets as remembrance. Hope to share your treasures to help others when the Spirit leads and provides timing and opportunity.

My sister, Sharol, called me after a women's gathering in her home, and she shared that a woman attending wanted her to tell me: "God is not withholding the water for harm but that the roots may go deeper still."

How amazing. God saw me in my need and spoke to a stranger who asked my sister to relay a message to me. I am so thankful to the Lord for impressing this woman and Sharol's love and obedience to make an overseas call to relay the message. The message was very timely; I needed encouragement.

This powerful word has helped me through many trials and was instrumental in breaking the lie of the enemy that battles or hardships were punishment.

May your roots go deeper still and the branch be forever connected, dependent on the True Vine, and fulfill your purpose mightily!

Journey on!

chapter 23

WHAT DO I WANT?
WHAT DO I NEED?
WHO AM I?

Oh, how many times questions cry out from deep within us. We have heard them many times and from many others.

Temporary satisfaction quells the hunger for knowledge. Then it returns, starving for answers. Oh, where does this search lead?

Are we adults trapped in a child's body seeking a loving family, a father, a mother who cherished us?

Are we lonely and desperately wanting friends or even a friend and we cannot seem to locate a true one?

Do we crave understanding, acceptance, comfort, and love?

Do we need help and direction?

A resounding yes to all of the above and many more questions and longings within!

We all need to know that we are loved that we have purpose, and that someone cares to know joy, peace, and contentment.

We need to recognize our uniqueness and our sameness but not elevate or lower one another through comparison.

We need to be excited about life and full of expectation.

We need to trust.

There is a way—there is One—not only an encounter or the dance—but rest!

We must continue in the acceptance of perfect love and wisdom from above to receive the inheritance that is here now and enjoy life in its fullness and purpose.

There is One who holds all the answers who is perfect in all of His ways and desires us!

He is Love, Compassion, Truth, Wisdom, Majesty, Power, All-Knowing, All Present, with no beginning or end. He is all that is *Good*!

He has been denied, ridiculed, blasphemed, ignored, blamed, and hated, and yet He remains the same. He desires, promises, and provides His best for us.

Oh yes, we must continue the journey to know, understand, love, and obey this One if we desire wisdom and to discover our true identity!

chapter 24

GROWING IN FAITH AND UNDERSTANDING

There are many traps or diversions present in life and in personal areas of interest. Involvement, support, and active participation are expected in your sphere of interest. This is part of responsibility as a member of a group or organization. Joy and pain are often intermingled with being singled out and noticed as one who has something important to say that provides insight or direction. However, sometimes, the tactic of shame (obligation) is pressure to meet or provide a need. This bridge must be crossed with eyes open, with each step taken with more resolve to discover truth and heed the call, or the warnings.

As one matures as a Christian and realizes personal limitations and recognizes common pitfalls, the walk is definitely difficult, yet it is full of hope and becomes easier. You discover a new direction, peace, and spiritual hunger, despite all the briars, you do not want to give up. It becomes easier to identify wrong attitudes that worm their way insidiously into lives. The new walk or way offers a channel of communication with the Creator of all Good and offers great insight and comfort, including continuous hope and forgiveness.

It is a new journey. However, I believe it is the beginning and a continuance of a preplanned journey. Earlier, I shared how I wrote and kept journals for many years. They are such a part of me learning how to travel on this enlightened path. I learned how to get up and start again, how to forgive, how to dry the tears, how to turn from the anger, the depression, the pride, the deep-rooted insecurity, the unworthiness and rejection, and to go on stronger yet weaker all at the same time. It is an amazing trip! I realized the choice is mine; it is always individual but with Divine Help once the course is embraced.

So many lessons taught, so many freedoms gained, so many God interventions, warnings, truths, insights—truly an amazing journey. One of these incidents happened at a group gathering where I was a leader and a renowned speaker was coming in. I was in the shower in my hotel room on the second floor when a frog jumped out of the drain, obviously almost boiled to death! I screamed, and my husband took care of the intruder, but all I could hear was "Do not go back to Egypt!" I knew it was a warning, but I did not fully understand. I was familiar with the story of the plagues in Egypt, with frogs being one of the plagues mentioned in Exodus 7:11, when Pharoh would not let God's people go. However, I did not entirely comprehend what the frog and warning meant.

> It is for freedom that Christ has set us free. Stand firm, then, and do not let yourselves be burdened again by a yoke of slavery.
>
> —Galatians 5:1, NIV

I knew that being set free was not the end, but to live in freedom and not be caught in any worldly or religious expectations, regardless of pressure. I realized that this is a continuous battle until He comes again.

It also caused me to recall a previous dream from many years earlier. In it, I saw a crouching, emaciated, naked man. The man's back was toward me. He was in a corner crying out desperately for forgiveness. It was a pathetic sight. He was struggling to reach up to God in his own way.

The Lord responded to his efforts by gently saying it has never been about man on his own being able to reach God with his actions. It is about God reaching down and coming down to lift you up. The man seemed to understand. Moments later, the telephone rang to tell me of the death of an immediate family member. My mother was with this individual who passed away, and she told me that he kept crying for her forgiveness and another family member's forgiveness in the room. This was the first time that I became aware of a dream that had significant meaning.

Years later, it was discovered that this man was a pedophile who had damaged many. Regardless of our sinful nature, when one is truly convicted and repents, there is forgiveness. Some of the ones affected are still healing. Some are powerful kingdom warriors. The dream spoke deeply to me about the kingdom of God and His interventions in mankind.

Each incident powerfully impacted me, and I knew that they were significant. I asked to be taught all that each meant and I am still learning from the frog (which symbolizes evil many times in Scripture) and the powerful love and forgiveness extended and displayed by the naked, broken man. Both have been protective and helpful revelations. I continue to recall them, and they are like warning signs in my life and precious treasures.

Not only is the Christian walk difficult with all its mess amid religion (and its demands for works). Then there is a glass house with so many shouting, "You hypocrite, you narrow-minded bigot, you foolish fool, no way. How can you believe that? What a crutch. Come on and wake up to the new century." We hurt one another, yet I am told in His Word: to forgive, to love, to not judge, to help those in need, and to think of others more highly than myself. How can this teaching be so resented and misrepresented? How could anyone think it is easy? It is not possible without Divine help. Nevertheless, when you have obeyed, it is so comforting and peaceful knowing that you have pleased Him.

Unfortunately, many judge without and within the Christian faith, and millions have been deeply wounded, have been deceived, or have believed lies spoken about them or to them. Some of both persuasions, pro-Christianity and those opposed to the Christian faith, have pushed too hard, and not in love or in the best interest of others. Instead, they promote their own agenda and timing, which is manipulative, controlling, and people-pleasing. The main goal is to prove a point: "I am right; you are wrong!"

Whatever happened to the well-known "Golden Rule"?

> So in everything, do to others what you would have them do to you, for this sums up the law and the Prophets (Matthew 7:12, NIV) and, you shall love your neighbor as yourself (Matthew 22:39, NIV).

How can we hate, tear apart, compare, judge so quickly and harshly, if we love one another as much as ourselves or our own? There would be more understanding and more opportunity to share, that would lead to more trust, if only we would follow the above two Scripture verses.

There are many things that I do not agree with, but as long as one is not in danger for life, physical or sexual abuse, there is time to establish relationship and understanding. If only we would take the time and wait. Instead, we so often jump straight to judgment and ignore the need to connect.

I have experienced deception in life. I have seen and felt pain and abuse, more than some, far less than many. There is no earthly scale to measure the pain of a soul. We all have battle scars. We have all been hurt. It is not advantageous to compare the debutant, the elites, the orphans, those who live on the streets or eat from the dump, not even those who sell their own bodies, abuse others, or commit horrific acts of violence. Do we have the right to condemn? There are legal routes for broken laws. We have incomplete insight. We each can help one another regardless of our station in life. It is frightening to know that the opposite is also true; we have great capacity to hurt one another. Oh, how much richer and fuller we would be if we would only learn from one another and choose understanding instead of judgment and trust a righteous Judge.

Yet we proclaim our own standards, our own rights to judge, hate, or condemn, and we do not want to wait or to seek to understand. We want things our way. The voices in the streets, riots, demonstrations, political agendas, and appeals many are effective, but many revert to anger, destruction, generalizations, revenge, prejudiced minds, and all kinds of evil. Each wants what he or she wants. Our way is right! Their way is wrong! Truth is smothered in the conflict instead of prevailing. Wrongs definitely need to be recognized and corrected, and accountability addressed. But so many times we rush ahead and encounter defense mechanisms in place like a shield, tempers rise, justification and blame are in full mode, and hearing and perception is difficult and for many impossible during the demand of the voice of "rightness" to be heard. The flames of justice or injustice are rapidly fanned, and the fire rages.

Who am I to say anything? All I know is I feel the pain. I ache for the resolution. I try to be who I am created to be. Giving up the "savior complex" that I can fix it, the attitude of "What can I do?" I have little strength, money, or status to make any difference. What I must do is adjust my thinking and my attitude. What is it that I am able to do regardless of how small it seems to others?

Recently, my husband and I made the decision to leave immediately after a close friend's husband's memorial and begin the nine-hour drive home to be with a dear neighbor who had just lost her loved one unexpectedly. It was a small thing we could do to honor each of their loved ones and to share their pain and grief. One was a heterosexual couple, one a lesbian couple, both in grief; I felt their loss and understood their pain.

I drove by my neighbor's home recently and stopped to get out and give her a hug and see how she was doing? She cried as I hugged her, talked with her, and was so thankful that I took the time to stop. I do not think the world has always treated her with kindness. Again, small acts to express value of the individual, remain attentive and alert for other ways to help.

I have to realize I cannot fix everything or please everyone. Nevertheless, I am able to help a little financially here and there, offer a place of refuge, food, childcare, or transportation to an appointment; take in a movie together, teach a class, or simply laugh or cry together. This is where I am free to be and not held captive by the judgments of others.

I anguish over tsunamis, earthquakes, tornados, divorces, human trafficking, abuse, poverty, corruption, infidelity, lies, betrayals, neglect, tragedies, disease, addictions, pornography, suicides, and so much more that wounds far deeper than one realizes. We pull together in crises for a short season to ease our consciences, but in the weeks, the months, and the years, we often are on another page while others remain in their prison.

How is one to fight the pain of it all, the overwhelming sense of inadequacy, the anger, the blame? It is a continuous battle within. That is when I must fight that old frog and not go back to Egypt, which represents evil as previously stated (from the biblical story of the plagues of judgment on disobedience when Pharaoh refused to let God's people go [Exodus

7:11, NIV]). I cannot fall into or embrace the helplessness I feel at times. I realize I need to acknowledge the One who has a plan that is good for all who will accept it and will provide His peace in the midst of every storm.

The battle to love and forgive and to move in love and forgiveness is strong. One may want to remain angry, to scream, to hit, to destroy some things, but this was the warning of the frog, do not go back to the old ways, indulging the flesh instead of a higher way. I can judge an act, actions, and situations as wrong, even evil, but I never have the right to judge a person in the way that a Holy God alone has the right and responsibility.

Anyone who thinks the Christian faith and walk are easy have never walked in my shoes or any Christian's shoes that I know. There is continual criticism, judgment, mocking, confusion, and misunderstanding by some who do not accept or understand the walk. Death to self and its desires is a painful battle. Nevertheless, the sweetest fellowship, honesty, love, hope, and compassion are evident on the path when in alignment with the Master's Plan, and it is an amazing journey.

So, what am I trying to say: We need one another. We each do have a part, and we can disagree but not condemn whole thoughts, ideas, or groups of people by our self-righteous need to be in control and right! I love that I have church-going friends, non-church-going friends, and friends of many nationalities, of many faiths, and of different ideals or standards.

As previously stated, I have been involved with a maximum-security women's prison ministry for approximately fifteen years. I have friends that I consider very wealthy and influential, and some on welfare and disability, and some incarcerated. Some have seen such horrors and others tended by servants. Oh, what joy to see beauty in each one and long for each one to become even more beautiful and free. This is my personal desire. Moreover, it is a battle, but it is one worth fighting.

Let's take a walk.

> In three words I can sum up everything I've learned about life: it goes on.
>
> —Robert Frost, 1874–1963

chapter 25

BEWARE OF COMPARISON

Life is like a game of cards. The hand that is dealt you represents determinism; the way you play it is freewill.

—Jawaharlal Nehru, 1889–1964

Comparison—what a trap awaits if we continually engage in comparison. It can lead one to feel inadequate or superior, jealous or self-righteous, and many other such opposites, but it is all so self-centered.

You wonder how far back this goes. Did Adam and Eve look around and compare the trees? Did Eve consider the words of the tempter and compare them with what Adam had shared with her? Adam was there with her at the tree, and the comparative rationale and questions must have been active in his mind, but it seems he did not correct, question, or caution his wife. What a path that established. The man did not confront the enemy, did not correct or protect his wife, and a course was set. Eve was deceived.

There are so many obvious mess-ups in the history of mankind, with none of us free or clean. I recall a story from Mark 3:1–3 (NIV). Jesus is in the synagogue where a man with a withered or shriveled hand was also gathered for the Sabbath. In the preceding verses, Jesus expounded about the Sabbath and offended the teachings of the religious leaders.

Some were gathered to accuse Him of breaking the law of the Sabbath, but He felt compassion for the man with the withered hand. He healed him. However, as he looked around at the ones trying to set a trap for him, he was angry and deeply distressed. I think He saw lack of compassion, legalism, pride, and perhaps much more in their hearts.

This grieved Him. In order to grieve, you must first love and care. The man with the deformed hand was healed, but the Pharisees (the religious leaders) went out and plotted how to kill Jesus.

Maybe you have heard the saying, that "we are all dealt a hand to play" or "play the hand that you are dealt." Well, this man in the story had a withered hand, which probably interfered with his livelihood. Some are born with many disabling handicaps, others in horrific circumstances. Nevertheless, each must deal with the life they have until change. Depression, anger, fear, blame, and on and on can consume you if you long for the good or easy life and compare it with others' circumstances. Awareness of others' situations can inspire you, but it can also open the door to jealousy, envy, and pitfalls of destruction.

Hope for someone to help and intervene is a powerful force, and this man encountered it. He did not know when or if he would ever experience such an intervention of healing and release. Those suffering usually also do not know when a life-changing event will come, but how crucial it is not to give up hope and succumb to hopelessness.

As we all wait for release or improvements in personal lives and circumstances, we must not only guard against negative feelings but also avoid the hardness of our own hearts. This is what upset Jesus more. The withered hand was healed instantly, but the hardened heart grew harder and birthed murder to instill and maintain the law.

So many things can lead to a loveless heart: blame, self-defeating talk, anger, self-righteousness, unforgiveness, fear, hate, comparison, and other harmful choices. We must wait in hope for change and guard our thoughts. It is not an easy task but a much better outcome in the long haul of life's journey.

How glorious and welcome the thought is that Jesus is not comparing me to anyone else. He sees me. He loves me. He accepts me. How marvelous to think of the intricate way I was formed in my mother's womb all by the deliberate design of my Abba Father. It is so beyond understanding.

> For you created my inmost being; you knit me in my mother's womb.
>
> —Psalm 139:13, NIV
>
> My frame was not hidden from you when I was made in the secret place.
>
> —Psalm 139:15, NIV

Oh, to think that the Holy Spirit counsels God's own, as He personally leads, guides, and grants specific understanding or information to draw them deeper into spirit abiding. It is so humbling, amazing, and powerful. It is a process, designed for those desiring and willing to become more and more like Him.

How awesome are your ways, oh Lord. You create, You see, You know, You love, You forgive. You are ever seeing, pursuing, leading, loving, and restoring your children. Praise is to You. Thank you. I love you and am forever thankful.

Lord, how do I translate this into words that will help others to know you? How can I help them see that you are not comparing them to anyone? Not only is there no comparison by You, but also no condemning us when we are yours or reminding us of our past errors but healing us from them. You want to remind us of whom You are and what You have done, are doing and will do and who we are in You. Yes, Lord, yes, help me to remain in this frame of thought and know Your Goodness and Faithfulness. You are an awesome God.

We wear ourselves out trying to do what is right, self-effort, or by running from You instead of to You. Nevertheless, you invite all, Lord, to come and rest in You. You are Life.

The beckoning to the dance—oh, I feel the call, I sense the joy, the expectancy, the rest. It is beyond explaining. What a banquet it will be!

chapter 26

POINT OF TRANSITION

To recognize the impact that the fruit of labor has in our lives we must revisit the birthing process. When the time has arrived for the life within the womb to come forth, a natural progression begins—early labor, active labor, transition, and presentation! The newborn has arrived.

As discussed previously, transition is the most critical time; the normally closed door (cervix) has made way for the child to enter the birth canal and to come forth with a future destiny.

The journey has not been an easy one for the mother, the infant, and perhaps not the father either. Change has occurred, and nothing will be the same again. There is no going back, only forward. From the moment of conception all has been leading up to the moment known as birth. Happy Birth Day. It is time to celebrate new life.

Labor is real. As it is in life, it requires work. We struggle, we strive, we hope, we dream. An idea is conceived, and we hope for its realization. Many never progress, many are disrupted or aborted, some are distorted or lost, but some dreams are realized. Steps to bring forth a dream are similar to childbearing, labor, and delivery.

The path to fruitfulness or realization of a goal is difficult. There may be little support for the goal. It may be resented, considered foolish, or simply judged as wrong! If the door does not open, the hope and dream can die. If things do not line up, the struggle is draining, and after long-repeated attempts, realization of the goal may become futile. Readjustments to the vision are necessary.

If only we could see the natural pattern of bringing forth life's goals or dreams, then the plan or pattern would be more discernible. Our ideas would dance in hope and purpose: perfect alignment, setting, provision, timing, advancement, and then the realization of our dreams fulfilled. If only the process would progress quickly and productively and explode into the wonder of our world.

A newborn does exactly that. Unfortunately, not into a perfect world but through a normal progression, even with all of the possible problems, there is a pattern. However, our ideas and our hopes have many obstacles and not such an identifiable pattern. This is where I transition in my sharing. There are patterns. I need to go to the One who knows the path fitted and suited for me. I need to seek the Master Planner if I want to be fulfilled.

I believe in the God of love who knows me, who desires my best, and who has good plans for me. He created me for intimacy with Him. I do not know how to share the joy of realizing this Truth that I am loved. It has taken me many years to realize I am not being compared to anyone else. Nor should I compare others or myself. Nor do I have to earn love or beg for it or for forgiveness. It is all within the boundaries He has provided and set for me. He is the perfect pattern maker.

There are many scriptures and powerful truths in the Bible that reveal God's finite design and involvement regarding creation, the giving of the Law, the construction of the Temple to include all the intricate fixtures with detailed instructions; how to make, assemble, and carry, and very explicit instructions for specific responsibilities. It is an amazing and fascinating record of God's relationship with His people.

I want to share the transition in me and I do not even know how. I know it is real, and it is not religious. It is Spirit. A relationship conceived in purity and holiness by a Holy Creator but so flawed by human effort. I am still pursued by a lover that will never give up on me. That is an exciting truth. I have become so much more aware of His Goodness and Presence.

I am still being taught and birthed into deeper awareness of acceptance, freedom, and rest. I am learning to embrace the moments. This is not easy.

Nor is it the world's way. I am learning to trust the hope within me and that it will progress to benefit others and myself as I walk with Him.

What joy to realize a dream and see it enjoyed by others. Precious are the fruits of labor. Often costly, but the joy and the reward is fulfillment! Rejoice for a while, adjust to the transition, and return to the waiting table where new hopes and dreams will be implanted.

If only we would go immediately to our Creator and trust Him for guidance instead of scheming and handling on our own, we would be further along in the renewal process. His Patience is the ultimate example of love.

I know how plans and dreams can be shattered. I have had my share and may have more, but I am learning a new and better way. The labor is hard, the obstacles are many, but there is an undergirding and inner knowing that it will be okay, regardless of expectations or outcome! There is so much more to see, to learn, and to experience in the wonder of His unfolding plan. I do not ever want to go back to independent me, trying so hard to fix everything and make it work! Persevere, but not alone and not without purpose.

All transitions, all changes affect us. I have a Helper, and it makes me different. I am thankful, I am secure, I am progressing in spite of all the hardships. I am favored. Yes, I am, and I hope that soon we can visit the dance that I mentioned earlier! On the other hand, He has an exciting encounter that He has personalized for you, but we will stop in momentarily and drink of the awe at the dance!

chapter 27

ONWARD

I have shared some of my thoughts and experiences, but each of us will continue our own unique journey. As alike and different as we are, we have much in common. Do we really know ourselves? Does the world or anyone know us?

Where do we find and possess our identity? Who is keeping count of all our mistakes and all of our successes? Is our scale balanced? Life is not a game. It does not have a huge scoreboard with all your stats being continually calculated, updated, and evaluated. No, life is not a game.

Thankfully, there is an answer, One who will reveal your identity, your uniqueness, your gifting, your strengths, your weaknesses, and your eternal purpose.

I have grown in my awareness of a loving Father who miraculously created me, knows me completely, and loves me totally. I know my Lord and Savior, Jesus, who gave up His royal position to show me the way back to the heavenly Father, by providing the way of reconciliation. He took all my guilt and shame, all my weaknesses, and loved me where I was and am. He continues to make a way for me daily.

The story is so amazing and so full of love and grace that I cannot begin to share it all. I know God has been pursuing me, seeking me, and calling to me always. He never gives up on me and forever desires a relationship with me.

His Presence is with me. His rod of correction has sustained me. His gentle voice has guided me. His Spirit has taught, convicted, comforted, encouraged, and empowered me.

I could never tell it all. I do not have the words to describe His involvement in my life, my world. It surrounds me, it encapsulates me, it frees me. It is amazing love. It is amazing freedom. It is amazing security.

I do know a book that will share the Power, the Glory, and the Story that will assure each of us of His goodness and His plan for our good. He is always aware, always available, and always able to complete His plan. The book is known as the Bible, the Holy Bible, Scripture, the word of God—alive and full of truth and wisdom.

Regardless of how many times we go round and round, slip and fall, ignore or delay interaction with our Father, His Son, and His Holy Spirit, He remains constant and faithful. He wants to interact with us. He knows everything about you and me and yet He loves us. What a safe and trustworthy God.

I cannot convince anyone of the reality of His Presence, His love, His plan, or His Existence. Only He can reveal Himself. The wonder of the unfolding of His love is indescribable. I am so thankful for His steady hand on my life. I am so grateful for His promise that He will always be with me guiding, protecting, sustaining me and He is *all* I ever need.

Why do we resist Him? Why do we listen to the world? Why do we ignore Truth and choose familiar far lesser avenues to achieve our goals? Foolish delays, unnecessary battles, and yet we trudge on fighting and rejoicing in our victories and drowning in our sorrows. There will always be joy and sorrow, but He wants to be partnered (yoked) with us carrying the load.

So many of His alive Words flood my thoughts, my very being, and I am able to rejoice regardless of the situation or circumstance. However, the times I falter in fear or grumbling, He reassures me and restores my peace and joy. His words are life. Please seek Him and read His story and His letters to you. Invite Him to reveal Himself. Ask someone to help you who knows Him intimately, for He desires to talk to you. Purchase, find, or ask for a Bible. Ask Him to help you understand, and be ready and excited about an amazing journey!

A simple invitation to know this God, His Son Jesus, and to be filled with His Spirit, begins with the acknowledgment that you are not perfect, that you have made mistakes and you want to know forgiveness and the assurance that He has an eternal reward for you.

Cry out, if you are real God, I want to know you and serve you.

Admit your mistakes (sin).

Ask for forgiveness. By an act of faith, accept forgiveness.

I believe in you, God. I believe that you sent your Son, Jesus, as my Savior, to die for my sins and take my punishment.

Please come into my heart, make me new, and fill me with your Spirit that I may serve you and walk in your Light.

Thank you for cleansing me, loving me, and claiming me as your own child.

> If you declare with your mouth, "Jesus is Lord," and believe in your heart that God raised him from the dead, you will be saved. For it is with your heart that you believe and are justified, and it is with your mouth that you profess your faith and are saved. (Romans 10:9–10, NIV)

Praise be to God Almighty if you have made the decision to believe in the gift of salvation (saved from our wickedness) and accepted Jesus as your Lord and Savior. You now have the promise of eternal life.

God has a plan and purpose for His children.

> But you are a chosen generation, a royal priesthood, a holy nation, His own special people, that you may proclaim the praises of Him who called you out of darkness into His marvelous light. (1 Peter 2:9, NIV)

The purpose of our life and its future destination depends on one thing and one thing only. Who do you believe Jesus is, and what do you do with that knowledge?

section 4

SEEING THROUGH A NEW LENS

*As I grow older, I pay less attention to what men say.
I just watch what they do.*

—Andrew Carnegie, 1835–1919

chapter 28

CRAYONS

The joy of a new box of crayons, the smell, the variety of colors, their sharp points, is exhilarating. Wow, it was a big box, with separate inner boxes. Such excitement! Pleasant memories from my childhood, and then expectancy, watching my children and then grandchildren's eyes express the joy of a new box of crayons. I was excited to share their discovery.

However, the terror of their little fingers breaking the crayons in half and peeling the papers off. No! No! No! Why do they do that? They held in their hands a new awakening, a small box of crayons, an exciting coloring book or construction paper. They were excited but not old enough or responsible enough to care for the ultimate "big box" appropriately yet. It was so difficult to see the crayons broken, naked without their papers or smashed down and dull after one short use! Where was the awe of the prestigious crayons in their box and the budding artist's originals?

Oh my, sometimes it is joy and at the same time difficult watching discovering little minds. I did not want to overreact, but they need their paper. They need to be whole. Oh my, calm down. It is okay. The tool remains, and with potential, for individual creativity. The page was quickly filled with a beautiful display of a gleeful child's artwork. The box and crayons do not need to be perfect. They will fit nicely in a plastic container, so much easier for little hands to handle.

Nevertheless, something in me shutters as I come back and find more papers on the floor or in the container. If that were the only stress to life, what a life it would be. They are enjoying freedom; I want order and perfection, if for a brief moment. The artwork is beautiful, but something constrains me and makes me feel a failure if the crayons are naked and broken. Did I not train up those in my immediate realm of responsibility right? Did I neglect responsibility? Oh, how easily thoughts can go introspective. It is just a box of crayons; however, mine are neat and on the shelf! Warning, do not return to human effort of perfection!

One evening, while I was at the prison, I thought of all the women from different backgrounds, economically, financially, racially, educationally, and age-wise. They were like a box of crayons. They were placed in the box at random but with set boundaries. Their exterior was the same color (all clothing alike) yet each so different. Each skin tone is beautifully unique, and their outer shell is not arranged by color, height, sharpness, brokenness, or nakedness. Many were broken, many were dull, and a few thought they were sharp, but you could see the flaws in their self-perception.

They had a quality that we miss so many times. Those who had been uncovered and broken were a head above those struggling to fit in. They were on the inside, establishing lines of cooperation. They were standing tall. Regardless of what they looked like on the outside, they had learned to live in a crayon box with dignity.

I thought how artists want sharp, ready instruments for their masterpieces. They tend to line up like colors and arrange them in compatible circles or lines. In relationships, many tend to surround themselves with like colors, thoughts, ideas, goals, and backgrounds. What a dull box, such limited variety and narrowness. Easier to get along with those of like-mindedness, but oh, what a rainbow you are missing.

Those incarcerated have a great opportunity to learn to live together under very difficult situations, and it has been amazing, watching and learning from their adaptability and growth. Do all of them gain this community of respect and beauty? Absolutely not! Do we? I have seen much compassion in the prison. Are we sensitive to the needs of others and not only our family or friends?

On the other hand, do our crayon boxes have to be perfect, sharp, in line, and on the shelf with the owner in control?

chapter 29

BACK TO THE CRAYON BOX

More to glean from the crayon box—oh, yes, we do not want to miss our parallels in real life. Originally all sharp, so beautifully lined up as a display (in a newborn nursery), equal, all secure, but about to face change. Life touches us.

Soon we will be in another's hand. Some of us will soon be worn down, broken, naked, abused, loved, cherished, forgotten, discarded, or even replaced. The original carton changes. What was a safe place may become a place of pain and torment, a dream palace, or anything in between.

Some may look perfect and standing so straight and tall, and some may appear rough and worn, but what if we could see beneath the exterior? "I am never picked. I am alone and not worthy." Other crayons may cry out, "Oh, please don't pick me again. I am so dull now. I have been smashed between strong fingers and pressed down so hard." Oh no, not only an abused and abandoned crayon, and now, here comes insecurity and comparison with the cry, "If only I could look like the one in the corner so straight tall and perfect!" How it parallels our thoughts as we look around a room. Which one are you?

So many times in life, we are not aware of the beauty of one's self, in the artist's—or the master's—hand. Pressures, changes, and vulnerability cloud the whole. We are not aware of our significance in creating a masterpiece. We fall into the despair of comparison. A vicious trap is set to rob security, joy, and satisfaction and instead foster pain, fear, and disappointment.

There are many parallels in our lives, workplace, homes, or appearance. The crayon box is a small indicator of our comfort zone and of our patterns. Is our desk or work area cluttered or our home? Is it in such an upheaval, that only you can hope to find something that you need or want after considerable effort?

Do you hang on to things that you have not used in years but may need, or do you discard quickly after the item has finished its service? Do you purchase used clothing or only top brands even if deep debt results? The image proclaims, "I must stay in top order" or "I have to get by as best as I can," and even accusations that scream, "I am not worthy of that experience or to own that item!"

We can know such heartache and disappointment when we embrace jealousy, comparison, and anger, and on and on it goes. It is like a rainbow of children full of life lined up to play a new game. The organizers, the bosses, the ones in control, quickly pick some out of the lineup, while others wait expectantly for their turn, their recognition, or their promotion. However, when the same scenario is replicated, pride and arrogance rise in some, despondency and failure in others. Some stand atop their own trophy while others try to hide and hang on to hope. We build barriers. The one always picked first, or is the artist's favorite, may become puffed up, but is at risk of toppling from the high place, and the fear of "Oh no, I am not number one now. What have I done wrong?" Hopelessness tries to take up permanent residence in those continually unnoticed.

However, hope may arise in the one never noticed, and maybe this will be the time of selection. Fear has taken hold at times in all of us. Fear is a fierce enemy of the successful and the ones longing for success. A cloud of confusion and comparison shrouds the truth, that each is wonderfully and creatively made, and with inherent value and purpose.

We are interesting creatures of habit. We have so much in common, but the thought of some things that we are not comfortable with or have never experienced scare us. However, we all are a part of a gigantic crayon-box-like system. We do all fit, and all are held on this planet earth by the same force, with common basic needs. Some are duller or less creative, some create flair, many search for more, and some are steady and content. Variety is exciting, and we need to enjoy it and not be intimidated by differences or shun, put down, or fear one another. Embrace the multifaceted beauty of difference and thereby enhance your life and your senses. It is like a smorgasbord; enjoy the beauty and creativity in you and others in our crayon box dwelling.

How do we honor and understand one another? How do we get beyond comparison, and all of its ugliness, that attaches itself and demands recognition? Some long for the perfect picture: "All of us equal and beautiful and at peace in our box." Where is purpose revealed and fulfilled? How do we get out of our boxes, those inherent, and those that we have created ourselves, blockaded in for safety? How do we shine individually and as one and display a massive masterpiece?

Oh my, it is time to pause and consider going to the dance. Why is there delay?

chapter 30

SEMI-TRUCK–
ACCESS POWER

I had a strange dream in the early spring of 2012. I was in the cab of a semi-truck straining to turn the wheel and make it out of a parking lot. It seemed to be a filling station, without hitting gas pumps, destroying curbs, cars, or anything else nearby. I made the turn successfully, but there was a huge hill right outside the area that I had just successfully maneuvered and exited. I was slowly rolling along when I noticed my brother motioning and yelling up to me. My two sons, who are grown, were on bikes racing alongside me, watching me in sheer wonder or horror. I was blocking traffic and coming to a stop; I could not seem to move. The truck is completely stopped dead, and here comes the *law*. As the officer addressed me, he requested to see my CDL (commercial driver's license). I had no CDL and not exactly sure of what one really was, but now I knew that it was required to drive an eighteen-wheeler.

Hum, I thought I could say the children did it, and I was trying to stop or correct the situation, knowing they were but children and the punishment would not be as severe for them. I would be justified in my actions. No punishment for their mother or any burden assigned.

My mind was in overdrive. No, I cannot do that! I cannot say that!

Commit to Change

However, it will be worse on you, rather on me, that is, if I do not come up with something quick. I cannot do it. What kind of mother tries to save her own skin and blame her children?

Wait! I never turned the key on. There was no infraction, or at least one not as great as driving without a license. No power was ignited. I was guilty of foolishness but not of breaking the law by driving without the big CDL. Oh, how quickly self-righteousness warmed me.

I ignored the warning of my brother, who is a skilled driver, who does have his CDL, as well as the look of shock on my children's faces. I lived for the moment in the thrill and achievement of my adventure. *Uh oh, caught.* As rapidly as the excitement had come, now fear, shame, and doubt all rushed in. Again, my racing mind was scheming. A loophole in the law invaded my thoughts. What a clever awareness that I had found. I was not driving without a license. I had not turned the key. Am I slick? What was my crime going to be? I was sure it would be less than the former implication. Such seeds of rebellion, self-protection, excuses, blame, and foolishness are rooted within and easily accessed.

Wait, why didn't I blame someone else? I knew that would be wrong, and it would definitely hurt my children to see their mother in such deception and lies. However, I was entertaining how slick it was to point out the non-driving status, just accidently coasting along and just an innocent mistake!

The so-called satisfaction was fleeting. I realized I was trying to maneuver a semi-truck in my own strength, with no power—how ridiculous—but it did provide a loophole for escape! Pride embraced me because I had made the turn without incident. Immediately, I shifted thinking of ways to excuse my behavior and folly by pointing the finger and shifting blame. How insidiously and rapidly fear and self-preservation invaded my thinking.

How many times in my life journey was I just coasting along on a wave or grasping another star? I needed to "use the power" as it was intended to be utilized, and within its boundaries!

I began to dissect this strange dream. The realization of the pattern of temptation took on a completely new meaning. It so parallels the Garden of Eden pattern. Partake in the temptation, try to hide, try to escape, blame, shame, and guilt with eventual accountability. Moreover, the cycle goes on.

More thoughts or insights considered about my truck-driving experience: Whether we are in a pit or on a mountaintop, just coasting along in life, struggling to tread water, feeling the undertow, running the race freely or feeling overwhelmed, it takes turning-on power to change position and to alter our course.

Use the power. Not just knowing power is available, but knowing it is for me and for you. It is provided and available in an immeasurable unending supply. Know the source and the effectiveness of rightly accessed power.

How do we obtain the power given to us? We do so by knowing it is ours, being aware of the arrangement and the conditions of its use and the source of the power.

Many times, we cannot use or accept the use of something due to ignorance, indifference, or foolish self-efforts. Eventually, we will break if we do not learn to access the True Source of Power.

I shared this dream with the female inmates at the prison that I routinely visit. They understood the implications revealed within the dream. They grasped the ideas of loopholes, shifting blame, and the thrill of the moments. However, more importantly, they acknowledged the great privilege of the Power that has been legally transferred to them with the acceptance and acknowledgement of who Jesus Christ is and what He has done at great cost for them. They realized they were granted legal access, rights, and expected use, with full benefits. Use the Power. What an awesome privilege and gift.

Rightly, use the power, accept it, and believe it is for you, and on goes the journey, but be fully equipped!

chapter 31

TRAPPED TO KILL, BOUND TO BE SET FREE

Saturday, March 12, 2017, in the wee hours of the morning, I was hurting and desperate to know how to help in the situation unfolding before me.

There was a huge metal trap, larger than a normal size male or female. It held a captive. The metal was inflicting pain and injury every time the captive tried to move or escape.

The individual was struggling and whimpering. There was such hopelessness. My heart was breaking. What could I do? Then I noticed a black hood over the captive's head. Blindness accompanied the pain and helplessness.

I cried out, "What can I do? I cannot release the powerful jaws of the trap. I am not strong enough." Every time the victim tries to remove the powerful jaws or struggles against the encasement, it increases pain, discouragement, fear, and all kinds of evil manifestations. Diabolical laughter and taunts fill the air.

"What am I to do? The helplessness is crushing me. I want to help. Look up! Trust! Believe! I know the One who is able! Yes, but what am I to do?"

In the quietness of my spirit, I heard, *trust, release, believe, pray*! Accept that some are not ready to come out of darkness. It is their familiar abode and they are afraid. It is easier to stay in the cover of darkness without seeing or hearing. I am there with them, and I am at work. I am never stagnant or never not present!

Trust and release. I will. I hear the cry. I feel the pain. Please move quickly on their behalf. For it is you alone who is able, and I stand ready to obey further instruction, I wait for your timing.

I was able to breathe a sigh of relief, for I was comforted and returned to sleep. My encounter was vivid and recounted with precision.

What amazing comfort and hope came my way a few days later in an email. I found it very interesting that it was delivered in the wee hours near the time that the dream had been revealed to me. It was a devotion by Anne Graham Lotz entitled "Bound in God's Will" that recounted the arrest of Jesus and the rough treatment that He sustained at the hands of mankind.

It is so amazing to ponder the Son of God, Co-Creator of all, Immanuel (God with us, Matthew 1:23, NIV) being mistreated, bound, and taken for trial and eventual crucifixion.

> In the beginning was the Word, and the Word was with God, and the Word was God. He was with God in the beginning. Through him all things were made; without him nothing was made that has been made. In him was life, and that life was the light of all mankind.
>
> —John 1:1–4, NIV
>
> The Word became flesh and made his dwelling among us. We have seen his glory, the glory of the one and only Son, who came from the Father, full of grace and truth.
>
> —John 1: 14, NIV

Jesus submitted to the will of His Father in the Garden of Gethsemane (Matthew 26:39, NIV) and thereby to the horrible ordeal that was ahead.

Anne Graham Lotz, in her devotion, also asked if any of us struggle with being or feeling bound, and if so, does struggling or fighting against what holds you cause you to experience more pain? We need to know God's leading in our battles. Sometimes, bindings are to be cut, and in other situations, we are to walk through the trial, not resisting the bindings. Pray for wisdom and understanding and wait for His guidance. Remember, Jesus was in alignment with His Father's purpose and obeyed.

What an inspirational moment for me. Both painted very powerful visuals in my mind. We have an enemy. I recall a verse in Scripture, John 10:10, NIV (words spoken by Jesus to religious leaders and Jews gathered).

> The thief comes only to steal and kill and destroy; I have come that they may have life, and have it more abundantly.

Oh yes, we experience many trials during our lives. Our response changes things; courses are established. We dig our own mud holes sometimes, other times unexpected and unrecognized traps may temporarily ensnare us. Our focus, our understanding, affects the outcome. There will always be pain and betrayal in this life, but we can grow and move forward stronger than ever if we align ourselves with the One who knows how and does work out all for our good; surrender to the True Deliverer.

Another Scripture or two come to mind.

> And we know that in all things God works for the good of those who love Him, who have been called according to His purpose. (Romans 8:28, NIV)

> Therefore, we do not lose heart. Though outwardly we are wasting away, yet inwardly we are being renewed day by day. For our light and momentary troubles are achieving for us an eternal glory that far outweighs them all. So we fix our eyes not on what is seen, but on what is unseen. For what is seen is temporary, but what is unseen is eternal. (2 Corinthians 4:16–18, NIV)

The battle in the mind relentlessly continues. The answer is to know and hold on to Truth in all circumstances and rest, trust, obey, and believe. Help is not only on the way it is ever-present!

I have not always been victorious in my battles, but am so thankful for the One who can turn my defeats into something beautiful!

I am thankful for the Promise-Giver and Keeper. I do not want to remain in defeat. Let hope arise and let us fight the enemy together. We have mountains to climb and obstacles to overcome, but we are not alone. Remember, Jesus was bound and yet in the perfect will of His Father.

Bound together with His cords of love and bound to be free!

chapter 31

ROADS

Life is full of many paths or roads. They vary immensely from time to time. Some are short; some are very long. They are frightening, exciting, challenging, or even horrifying at times. Some paths are fun, joyful, and rewarding, while others are boring, overwhelming, or disappointing. At intervals, they may be lonely, and at other times very overcrowded. Of course, you can be alone, feel satisfied or completely surrounded by others, and be extremely lonely.

These paths start early in life and continually change and challenge you all along your advancing years. You cannot predict them or change them, only respond to them.

Responses come in varying degrees also. You can run and try to get off quickly, or you can linger to enjoy, or make no progress at all. We can get bogged down one time or another, or wastefully hurry our way, and miss the lessons on the roadway.

There are many reasons, we seem to travel the same roadway repeatedly. We must be missing the purpose and its importance in our personal destiny. If we fail again, we will revisit the training ground until the lesson is grasped. We require a faithful and steadfast trainer.

We should be like a lamb following the voice of the shepherd, trusting that his crook will snatch us and keep us from harm. However, like the lamb, we like to frolic and play or resist and drag our hoofs! What a patient and wise shepherd is needed.

If we will, only let wisdom and truth guide us. We must seek it and wait for it. We must accept that we do not have all the answers, and neither do those around us. Wisdom and truth will lead and guide as His Light illuminates our path.

Speak to yourself, please slow down, and trust. Stop trying to figure everything out and storing information and things in neat little boxes. Wait, quiet your thoughts, listen intently, and wait for the light. It is difficult not to be self-sufficient, or more accurately, to admit that you do not have all the answers or know how to handle everything. We cannot completely control our surroundings or those of fellow travelers in life. We often find ourselves in quite the predicaments. What are we to do?

I fondly remember the dance. I would like to tarry there again. Maybe now is the time for you to hear about the time on the dance floor. I know there is a dance saved for you!

section 5
THE INVITATION

Beware of missing chances; otherwise it may be altogether too late some day.

—Franz Liszt, 1811–1886

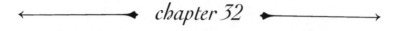

chapter 32
THE DANCE

Enter with me a large, dimly lit room. Many people are in the room, but there is no motion. I look around. Some are whispering at the edges of the room, along the walls. I realize that I am in a ballroom. I am not comfortable dancing. I am awkward and have never been free enough to dance without being self-conscience.

Then I am asked to come away from the wall. I heard my name whispered, and I am instructed, "Do not be afraid. Come out from the others and come to the center of the room." Strangely, I was not afraid. The Voice was so gentle and full of love.

He takes my hand, and we lightly glide around the room. Everything and everyone disappears, and it is just the two of us.

I was enveloped by an intensity and depth of love and acceptance that I had never known. I was filled with awe and wonder. The dance is over. I slip back to the edge, automatically back into the crowd. However, no longer the same, I feel alone yet not alone, a little lightheaded but full of hope and anticipation for the next dance.

Time passes, a few years go by, and a second time, I see myself on the dance floor. My lover is calling. Maybe it is time you meet Him. His Name is Jesus. He is slowly turning me as we glide effortlessly over the dance floor. Again, His wonderful peace envelops me. His love surrounds me and fills me, as before, beyond experience or imagination.

This time, I notice as He turns me, there are arrows in His back. He is turning me so that He can protect me and take the brunt of the attack. A few hit me. He is very aware and looks intently in my eyes, and I know that He has given me all that I need, to not only withstand but also to overcome the attacks. He is absorbing many arrows to my one, but He never dodges or flinches. Love is tangible. He is *love*. I am at peace and rest in His embrace.

Even when I long to join Him on the dance floor, I must wait to hear my name. It has been years again. It is not a painful delay, for there are many precious encounters, but I do long to revisit the ballroom. The remembrance of the previous encounters is enough, but a sweet desire to join Him again lingers deep within.

I am invited for a third dance. It begins slowly and familiarly, but suddenly, Jesus dips me low to His side and *roars* like a *lion*. I see a huge javelin or spear hurling violently towards me. At the sound of His roar, it shatters and drops to the dance floor. It crumbles and falls powerlessly at the sound of His Voice. As I was tipped down, I had a clearer look at His back. His flesh revealed the severe scourging and punishment that He had chosen in love to endure for me. The Gentle Lamb, the Good Shepherd, gently holds me, leads me, and pulls me upright again. I dance with the Lion and the Lamb.

Again years pass, in the month of August 2016, it is time for the fourth dance. However, something is different. I am in a new place—I cannot see Jesus. I sense His Presence leading and holding me, but I cannot see Him. There is a bright light within me. There is an assurance of His full power. A new awareness of confidence and of His abiding power within is encasing me. A commissioning to carry forth His Presence, like never before, saturates me. There is a definite awareness that there will be dark times ahead, but the order is to trust in His light, His power, His name, and His love. He will direct my steps.

The once-insecure, hesitant dancer is able to spin and spin with so much joy, hope, and freedom. Self-consciousness eradicated through Father-Son-Spirit consciousness! The acute awareness that I am in a new place remains. A heightened awareness of my identity, not only mine but available for all His heirs is coming and is already here! His Presence forever, never to be diminished, more powerful than anything many have ever experienced as His Church, is accessible now.

The Lord-King-Majestic One within carries us to the ends of the earth. There is no turning back. He is coming in Power to His servants for the fulfillment of His plan and in preparation of His return.

The unfolding of His love and beckoning to me came over the years and was not the only intimate times with Jesus. I know there has been great truth, wisdom, and preparation revealed throughout the centuries and at different levels. For me, the dance is unique and holds much beauty and revelation of who He is, who I am, who the body of Christ is, His presence that leads and empowers us.

There was a great sense that the next dance, or last phase, will be at the marriage feast of the Lamb. Joy is unspeakable and inexpressible. Twirling exuberantly with laughter and freedom, all sorrow, pain, and grief are gone forever. Completion- united with Him for eternity!

chapter 33

THE TIMING OF THE DANCE

Whenever my world or thoughts spin out of control or seem wound so tight that explosion is inevitable and I cannot think how to prioritize, I remember the dance. It comforts me. I do not know which dance I am in or where it is, but as I stand on the dance floor and acknowledge His Presence, tension exits my body with every breath. Peace fills every cell. I am enveloped in love, and I am in awe. Time stops, and there is an absence of fear, with no awareness of time or space. Immediately a sense of rightness, completeness, and of being where I am meant to be envelops me. Peace and awe fill me.

How do I get to the dance? How do I remain? I have known the joy of the dance, but I know when I must exit. Even when I want to remain but must leave, the memory lingers and is so complete. Sometimes, I merely close my eyes and think of the encounter, and am surrounded by His Presence. I wait for the invitation to dance, and I am ready to move onto the floor. I am aware of a sweet fragrance, an overwhelming sense of love and acceptance, the memory or vision of the encounter sustains me, and I am empowered to move on.

In the natural, I am not a dancer. I am both awkward and self-conscious, thereby a very uncomfortable thought originally. It is not an encounter that I would choose to bring comfort. Why was I drawn to a dance floor, filled with such joy, and made aware of the price Jesus has paid and His desire to dance with me? How can it be? Yet another area of struggle addressed.

How does every weight drop off and disappear? How does every thought melt? I am moved gently around the room, only the two of us in the room, which only moments ago was filled. How is it that the focus is on me when so many desire and long for the attention? Somehow, I know the dance is for all, but how is it so personal, deep, and pure? It is so beyond every human joy, emotion, and intimacy, and impossible to fully relate or describe.

I long to return to the dance floor, but I am content in our precious times together. There is always a wooing to come apart and abide in Him.

chapter 34

REFLECTION

The mere connotations of the word reflect and the act of reflecting is a powerful asset as one looks back and seeks deeper understanding.

One of Webster's definitions of "reflect" is "to think quietly and calmly, to realize and or consider."

Reflection is described in part as the return of light. I understand the saying that hindsight is 20/20, that you can see more clearly in time. However, this is not always true.

We have all heard of resentments and hate that only grow deeper over years and spread throughout families or organizations, so what is the key to breaking the cycle? What gives light and understanding to the past?

The first definition of "reflect" in *Webster's Collegiate Dictionary* is "to turn away from a course."

Linked with the abovementioned definition, from the same source, to think quietly and calmly and turn away from an ungodly course is a big key. It is a search for understanding and truth, not judgment, blame, excuses, justification, or rightness. It is an act of surrender to search for truth and understanding. It is allowing light to come into the situation.

I believe the practice of reflection helps lead to the victories or breakthroughs in life's journey. There are many incidences and actions that we are unable to see clearly or comprehend, but there is hope that will sustain us, encourage us, and set us free. The ability to see through different lenses and gain understanding is the beneficial and desired outcome.

How many times do questions cry out from within? Why did this happen? Why should I? What do I want? Who am I? Does anyone care? What is wrong with me? Do I need help?

Sometimes one feels like a scared child and wonders if they will ever get it together in an adult world. Will there ever be a wonderful friend, relationship, or a marriage that is lasting?

We all crave to be loved, accepted, and to know our purpose in life, to know joy, peace, and contentment. We are each unique and alike in so many ways but do not want to be trapped in comparison. We should be excited about life and full of expectations. We need to trust.

We have been through quite a maze. Whether on the merry-go-round, in the crayon box, or a puffed-up attitude like the king of the mountain, or the lowly worm dragging along, we have shared some emotions. The adventure continues, whirlwinds will come. Stagnation will tempt you, but endure and carry on.

Such memories and gratefulness fill me. This has been cathartic for me, and I know that all is being woven into a masterpiece by the Master's Hand to transform me into His likeness.

What an amazing process and idea. He searched for me, He never gave up, and He pursued me with an unending love before I even knew Him. He is faithful to complete all that He has begun.

> Being confident of this, that He who began a good work in you will carry it on to completion until the day of Christ Jesus. (Philippians 1:6, NIV)

The battle to press through roadblocks and lead a productive life is difficult and frustrating at times, but it is active training. We need perseverance to stay the course and stand! There is always a way and help. He has promised never to leave us or forsake us, and to provide all we need to be an overcomer.

All of these promises and words of hope are in His word, known as the Bible. He is the One who holds all the answers, knows the whys, the truth, and is perfect in all of His ways.

He is mocked, ignored, denied, blamed, hated, and rejected, yet He remains the same. I must continue the journey to know Him more, and to know Him more is to love and trust Him.

He has promised to come again. Just as in the dance, I recognized the Lamb and the Lion. He will not come back as the gentle babe born in a manger but as the King of kings with a roar that overcomes all evil and claims His own.

Yes, I must obey this One! He is worthy of all love.

Stand firm until He comes again and takes us home to be with Him forever.

section 6

MORSELS AND NUGGETS

Knowing is not enough; we must apply. Willing is not enough; we must do.

—Johann Wolfgang von Goethe, 1749–1832

chapter 35

PIT STOPS

Through the years, life takes us many places, and often, there are hidden traps or pits along the way. You may have been in the roost where "birds of a feather flock together" as the cliché goes, with the aid of common opinions being shared with satisfying agreement. Such gatherings are limiting, even if some good comes from them, but many times it supports stunted views and negativity, thereby feeding judgmental attitudes. You must climb out of this nest, if no one is there to throw you out like the Mother Eagle, or you will never soar.

Another safety net appears, and one may camp out at "Que Sera, Sera" (sung by Doris Day, c. 1950). Perhaps not as comfortable as the likeminded friends, but you have resigned yourself to what will be will be, and you have nothing to do but exist and watch life go by. Never could enjoy this phase longer than a few minutes, but I have met many participants over the years. If only we hear, a clarion call, sounding come! There is a better way, a new and safe place to refresh, to learn, and to mature in wisdom.

I know the Voice. I have heard the call many times. I also know that there is no way to convince another to hear. No one can earn an invitation. He always desires for us to come into relationship with Him, and He pursues us relentlessly. He loves with an unimaginable love.

We have a Father who is perfect. He is the Creator of all that is good.

His plans for His creation are good. He is all-knowing (omniscient), ever-present (omnipresent), and with all power and authority (omnipotent). He does not just love; He is Love. There is no evil in Him; He is Holy, Holy, and Holy Lord God Almighty. He is the Master Planner. A Father who knows and sees all, and He loves unconditionally!

In His plan to restore relationship after rebellion against Him occurred, He came down from the heavens in human flesh, as His Son, Jesus (Yeshua), and lived among us. Displaying the glory of the Father, completing the plan of redemption, Jesus (through His horrific death and glorious resurrection from the dead) opened the way through His acceptable sacrifice for reconciliation with our Creator. Chains were broken, lives restored, and the door was opened wide to reconnect all with the Father, who accept His plan for eternal life. He purchased our freedom, took our punishment upon Himself, and secured many promises to those who accept, believe, and trust Him.

His Holy Spirit comes to comfort us, to lead us and guide us into all truth. As the revealer of truth and power, He helps us to lay down the chains that have been broken off of us, and to walk in the purchased freedom. Let go and soar. Oh, how I need Him every second of every day. The Holy Spirit emboldens us.

How my heart is stirred as I try to share about this new family. It is amazing; I have been adopted. I long to know Him more and all my family that is in Him. It is beyond understanding, but I know it is a good and perfect gift. I desperately want more, all, to become His family member.

There are so many words that fill my mind, heart, soul, and spirit from His word, but the search is individual. He is so longing for each to come. He wants to open and deepen the relationship with each one of us and to pour out His goodness on us. Come read, come abide, come listen, and partake of the Living Water and be satisfied.

May we journey on in His path, prepared individually for us. We are not alone. We are not judges. We are sojourners in this temporary homeland. There is great unspeakable joy and hope for those who say yes to His Voice and take His hand. Come on, let us enjoy life, and run a good race. The family that is destined to walk together as one, may we lay aside whatever hinders us, and take the first step in unity.

For every need, every situation, there is an answer. Maybe someday we can look together in His word. He holds the answers, the hope, peace, and encouragement. He is all we need now and forever. He has erased our past mistakes and is ever granting us a clean slate, as we trust in Him. Our past does not limit or define us; we are cleansed and a new creation.

My heart overflows with love and thanksgiving. I deserve nothing but punishment, and yet, He set me free.

Thank you for sharing part of my journey and may your encounter with the Lord be on the ski slopes, on the waves, or in the privacy of your home, or wherever He invites you to join Him. The dance was beautiful, and I look forward to whatever rendezvous is ahead for you and me!

chapter 36
I AM SIGNIFICANT!

Before I knew or accepted His love, the sheer magnitude of numbers, years, size, and complexity of the universe and its inhabitants since the beginning of time drove me into insignificance. How quickly we can be drawn or sucked into wrong focus. To think, no way can God be aware of me when there are approximately 7.4 billion people alive on earth today! Nevertheless, a real wow when you know He loves, cares, and is aware of everything. He is an amazing God and the One that I choose to serve.

*I am not insignificant. I have never been—am
not now—or ever will be insignificant.
I am significant! You are significant! We are significant!*

We are created by a loving Father who overshadows us with His love and care, who continually pursues us for relationship, and also protects and provides our needs. We live for His Glory and purpose. He is the creator of all that is good and keeps His word and promises and will eternally.

I have met His Son, who purchased me out of my debt and paid it in full. He suffered and died to rescue me, and His gift was accepted as a perfect payment. He secured a place for me with Him in His Kingdom. He declares me clean, whole, adopted, and righteous in Him. *What amazing love!*

Jesus, together as one with His Father, sent His Holy Spirit to comfort, guide, teach, empower, anoint, and fill the ones willing to receive with Himself and His nature. The Holy Spirit is stirring the family of God and quickening us to prepare for the reunion, the return of Jesus as King of kings. His own will spend eternity with Him.

Amazing love, there is no other reason. How humbling. I do not deserve—nor does anyone—such love and position in Him. It is His plan. Do I still struggle with the weight of all the pressure, pain, pride, and temptations of this life? Yes, but I know who is my help and who is able to deliver from *all* evil. Therefore, my battles are very different now. I am being changed more and more into His likeness (even though I cannot always detect), but that is what His Word says, and He has proven Himself faithful. I know He is Truth and Life. What a different journey. It may be a narrow path but not narrow-mindedness. It is so full of love, mercy, grace, truth, empathy, encouragement, hope, direction, correction, wholeness, and joy—true freedom!

It is not within my ability to convince you or anyone to change their mind or direction. I have tried to share who He is to me and to reflect Him. He says His children are like salt and light. I hope that some hunger and thirst have been stirred and activated to shed his light into darkness and despair. I hope that you have felt the yearning within, by His Spirit, to seek Him. Seek Him, and you will find Him, and we will continue on the paths before us.

I love you and really do want us to be together forever! Thank you. We are amazing because He is!

Some Closing Thoughts

We have run through a maze with many twists and turns. Whether on the merry-go-round, in the crayon box, the puffed up better than thou, or a whiner in a whirlwind or in a stagnant pond, the adventures continue.

What memories and thankfulness should permeate all of us. Since conception, we have been pursued by the Master to come to Him.

What an amazing process. He is faithful to complete all that He has started. He searched for me; He pursued me before I ever knew Him.

> The Lord your God is with you, He is mighty to save. He will take great delight in you; He will quiet you with His love, He will rejoice over you with singing.
>
> —Zephaniah 3:17, NIV

The battles to secure desired outcomes and press through the roadblocks in life is, at times, difficult and frustrating, but it is active training for life. We must persevere and stay the course to be able to stand. Stand until He comes again, and He will take us to be with Him forever in His kingdom.

Before I was a Christ believer, I had many wonderful friends and relationships with joys and sorrows along the path of life. However, there is no comparison of the greatest experiences before Christ was in my life with the fellowship and intimacy that is now real. It surpasses all relationships; it is truly unconditional love and filled with amazing plans, promises, and future rewards. The family of believers has also provided and opened new depths of family. It is impossible to describe, but it is an amazing family.

For a simple review before I say goodbye, I would like to share a key that helped me unlock the door to freedom. You need to acknowledge the hunger for change and growth, let go of the past, and live in the present as you look forward to the future with joyful anticipation.

1. Embrace the desire for change that is within you.
2. Open your heart and mouth, and speak out when appropriate. *Silence* is an accomplice of evil, and it grants power over you when it remains unchallenged.
3. Share with someone what it is that you want to be released from, and be set free. This person needs to be trustworthy and maintain a life that reflects victory. This opens you to vulnerability, so choose wisely.
4. Rejoice and accept that no one, no human, can cleanse your spirit and heart. But praise be to the One, Jesus the Christ, who fully identifies with our pain and was tempted in all things yet was without sin. He became the acceptable sacrifice to restore us, cleansed and whole to the Father and redeemed us unto Himself and His kingdom.
5. Release and let go of brokenness, anger, hate, unforgiveness, all wounds, and pain through the power of Jesus. Speak the release(s) aloud, one at a time: In Jesus's Name, I release_____ (fill in the blank), receive forgiveness, and extend forgiveness. Now, Lord Jesus fill those places that have been released to You, and cleansed by You, with Your love and Holy Spirit—for Your Glory.
6. Look at His nail-scarred hands—the only scars that we will ever need to embrace to obtain our healing, release, restoration, renewal, and adoption. What amazing love, grace, and mercy displayed and available to all!

Cry out as King David did in Psalm 51 when he acknowledged his sin and the need for cleansing.

Have mercy on me, O God, according to your great compassion blot out my transgressions. (v. 2) Wash away all my iniquity and cleanse me from all my sin. (v. 7) Cleanse me with hyssop, and I will be clean; wash me, and I will be whiter than snow. (Psalm 5:1–2; 7, NIV)

Every scar has a story and is associated with pain and a wound.

Every pain has a victory waiting or already celebrated, with the potential of ushering in your new identify.

Every life has a purpose known or waiting for discovery.

Every word has a sound and an ear to hear. Consider carefully your words.

Guard your thoughts, your heart, and your tongue.

May our testimony be an Honor unto our Father God, Our Lord and Savior, Jesus, and to the Holy Spirit. Lead us Holy Spirit and be glorified: the great three in one!

Thank you for taking the time to walk and share the journey with me for a short time. May our encounters with almighty God, be filled with awe and wonder and amaze others and ourselves as we share the experience. May we lead others to the nail-scarred hands that heal, deliver, restore, and open the door of eternal glory.

Let us journey together on the path before us and be forever united as One in His kingdom. What joy awaits us! May we be strengthened and encouraged in Him and continue in boldness and joy.

Until we meet again, I pray for you to abide in the true vine and bear much fruit for the kingdom.

It Is Time

His joy, His peace, His strength, His love, His comfort, His deliverance, His forgiveness, grace, mercy, kindness, healing—all of His attributes and character are available in the darkest of times, in the most painful of times, in the greatest loss or grief, in the greatest gains and blessings, in the wondrous joys and victories of our lives! He is there, and all is available. We are not always aware or do not acknowledge or accept Him or His gifts to us, but He remains.

To become more like Him, more Christ like, does not have an age or time limit. We are ever being changed into His likeness once we have accepted Him as our Lord and Savior. He is faithful to complete all that He has begun in us.

> Being confident of this, that He who began a good work in you will carry it on to completion until the day of Christ Jesus.
>
> —Philippians 1:6b, NIV

May we exchange or trade the old ways for new ways to obtain deep-rooted answers and needs that are inherent in all of us.

There comes a time when you are to close the cover on a book, close a door to the past or to walk away from darkness to Light. It comes to every one of us, and a move is in progress. Choose wisely. Our next step does make a difference, and sometimes it is an eternal difference.

Our pasts, our mistakes, and our accomplishments are never the end of the journey. We can choose to let it define us as to who we are, but it is definitely not the whole.

Regardless of the past, it is not our defining moment. Escape the condemnation, the judgment and waltz into your new identity. He is waiting with open arms, and what doors He shuts no man can open, and what doors he opens, no man can shut.

> I will place on his shoulder the key to the house of David; what he opens no one can shut, and what he shuts no one can open.
>
> —Isaiah 22:22, NIV

There are examples in God's word, when He shuts doors to protect and when He shuts doors to exclude. When Noah was obedient and built the Ark, by the exact instructions provided and procured all the provisions needed for the animals and his family, God shut the door. All inside remained safe and came forth out of the Ark.

When John the revelator saw heaven, he says,

> And into the city will be brought the glory and honor of the nations. But nothing unclean will ever enter it, nor anyone who practices an abomination or a lie, but only those whose names are written in the Lamb's Book of Life.
>
> —Revelation 21:26–27, NIV

I long for that day when I will be welcomed into His eternal kingdom. The only book that matters then will be His Book of Life. The trials, disappointments, battles, and wrongs will continue until that day. But my hope, faith, and walk, long for the open door into His kingdom.

> I am the gate; whoever enters through me will be saved.
>
> —Jesus's words; John 10:9a, NIV

Our future depends on who we say Jesus is and how we choose to recognize and walk in our days. It is an ongoing decision with permanent results.

However, this is not just for the future. Joy, assurance, peace, and the Presence of a Holy God with us in life is beyond human description and so very comforting. A life filled with peace, hope, and expectation is for now. All the pain and suffering, you come to realize, is part of changing us into His likeness, all the victories and joys, part of giving Him honor and Glory, as we release all claim.

It is not a crutch; it is not an empty hope or promise. No everything in the here and now physically is what will be totally gone one day. Believers are not exempt from heartache, disease, loss, or pain here on earth, but the difference is, as Paul says,

> To be absent from the body is to be present with the Lord.
>
> —2 Corinthians 5:8, NIV

When a young believer named Stephen was being martyred by stoning (after his proclamation to the Jews about their errors of who Jesus was), he gave the following account according to Scripture as he was filled with the Holy Spirit:

> Look, he said, I see heaven open and the Son of Man standing at the right hand of God.
>
> —Acts 7:56, NIV

> While they were stoning him, Stephen prayed, Lord Jesus, receive my spirit. Then he fell on his knees and cried out, Lord do not hold this sin against then.
>
> —Acts 7:59, NIV

I have chosen to serve this God, His Son, and His Holy Spirit, who are One, and I long to see Him face to face when He calls me home. I have never known such love and contentment since accepting Jesus, my Savior, who fully paid my ransom. It is an exciting daily journey and search to know Him more. Nothing compares to Him. Nothing can fill the void or provide all I need every moment of every day, except Him!

So the time has come for the covers of this little book to be closed. My hope and prayer is for each of you to continue the journey of seeking to know Him more. There are many helps available. Search for verses in the Bible that help with confusion, anger, unbelief, death, or any area that your soul is troubled by and needs help and answers. He holds the answers. What a feast and joy to discover. I look forward to meeting you someday.

> Don't judge each day by the harvest that you reap but by the seed that you plant.
>
> —Robert Louis Stevenson, 1850–1894

About the Author

Neva Welsh has spoken at meetings, conferences, churches, prison ministry meetings, youth gatherings, and small groups across the United States and in Germany and the Netherlands. She has insightful lessons in life to share from her personal background. She comes from a wonderful middle-class family that had some hidden secrets, like most families.

Over the years, she intervened with families experiencing challenging issues (i.e., child abuse, alcoholism, drug abuse, physical abuse, and dependency). She is very sensitive and aware of the effects of behavioral patterns on individuals and family members.

She often shares personal trials and the battle to fight through to victory. She is skilled at combining truths with her years of experience as a wife, mother, an RN, case manager, nursing supervisor, patient advocate, physician advocate, leader of study groups, leader of prison ministry meetings at a women's maximum-security prison and an Aglow International Regional Prison Ministry Coordinator.

She is comfortable with people across all spheres of education, economics, and racial barriers. She is a capable speaker and coordinator of events. She has served in leadership positions locally, statewide, and regionally in secular and Christian settings.

She is happily married; she and her husband have four married adult children and are blessed with grandchildren and recently great-grandchildren. She and her husband continue to enjoy travel and family gatherings.

Printed in the United States
By Bookmasters